Movin' On Out

MOVIN' ON OUT

Starting Out on Your Own—A Guide for:
*finding that first apartment
*polishing consumer smarts
*managing your money
*meeting new friends
*and much more!

David J. McIntyre

G. P. Putnam's Sons/New York

Library of Congress Cataloging in Publication Data

McIntyre, David J., date.
Movin' on out.

Bibliography: p.
Includes index.
1. Young adults—United States—Life skills guides.
2. Consumer education—United States.   I. Title.
II. Title: Moving on out.
HQ799.7.M29   1984   640   84-8305
ISBN 0-399-12974-X

Design by Constance Sohodski

Printed in the United States of America

Acknowledgments

The development of a book involves the interaction of many people, far too many than space allows me to list. However, I am particularly indebted to a number of people whose contributions cannot be ignored.

First, to the many people who have shared living-on-their-own experiences so they could be utilized in this book.

Second, to my friend and colleague, Edward L. Jones, without whose generosity this book never would have been written. Also, to Beverly Bisignaro, who wove a special word processing magic that saved countless hours and permitted me to meet deadlines.

I am also grateful to my agent, Astrid B. Seeburg, for her help, long friendship, encouragement and belief in the concept.

To Ron Green of the Putnam Publishing Group, for recognizing the potential of the idea and having faith in it, and to Judy Linden, my editor, for her guidance and encouragement, I offer sincere thanks.

My appreciation goes as well to several people who provided critical evaluation and protected me against error: Everett D. Randall, CLU, CPCU, AIU, of the Insurance Institute of America, Malvern, PA; John Fisher, CLU, ChFP, Northwestern Mutual Insurance Company, Media, PA; Philip A. Farley, Manager, Regulatory Assistance, Federal Reserve Bank, Philadelphia, PA; and, Glenn A. Yeager, Esq., Compliance Officer, Meridian Bancorp Inc., Reading, PA.

I am grateful for additional assistance provided by Gloria Farrow, Manager, Community Affairs, Allstate Insurance Company, Valley Forge, PA, and Sara Griffin, Public Relations

Department, Thomas Jefferson University and Hospital, Philadelphia, PA. Thanks, as well, for assistance from Judy Castaldi, Director, Fordham-Paige Clinic, Radnor, PA, and Jane C. Nickels, RD, Director, Food Services, Villanova University, Villanova, PA.

Ann Granat provided help with research at a critical point, and the staff at the Chester County (PA) Library, without knowing it, helped immeasurably to fill holes, provide access to facts and, in general, make my research task easier.

Special recognition should be made of the contribution of my parents, Erna and Gordon McIntyre, whose love of the language and whose example and interest helped me develop what level of competence I may have as a writer. To my wife, Glenda, who saw little of me over many months, but who supported my efforts with boundless enthusiasm and encouragement, I am forever grateful.

To Karen D. Chambliss and David R. Chambliss, two people who have been a very significant part of my family over the past eight years. As they moved on out, their efforts and exploits, successes and mistakes, provided the idea for and the impetus behind this book.

Contents

Movin' On Out: An Overview

This year, over 4 million people between the ages of eighteen and twenty-six, from greatly varying backgrounds, will set out on a common odyssey. They, like you, are "movin' on out," to form a new and independent life, away from homes known since childhood.

The reasons are many: to seek fame and fortune, accept first full-time jobs, marry or establish a living relationship outside marriage, get away from parents or siblings, declare independence.

For whatever reason, this ritual takes place each year, and it sets off a chain of events, activity and decision making that is shared by all who make the break.

It is a time of movement. It is moving *on* to something new. Perhaps most important, it is moving *out*; away from the relative comfort and security of what has been—and in some cases will remain—home. The individual is moving out to a new home, his or her first home as an adult, be it ever so humble.

For some, the move is a few blocks or a few miles, still within safe distance of "home." For others, it is where the jobs are, in cities of all sizes. To still others, the move can be across the country or an ocean.

There is some comfort, perhaps, in knowing that additional millions have traveled the path before you. Most have made the adjustment quickly and have settled into their lives with a minimum of distress. Some returned home, done in—if only temporarily—by the problems they encountered. They were, for the most part, unprepared. Most try again and succeed the second time, somewhat wiser for the experience. A few will never make it.

Here are some things that may be helpful in making your move. Much of the information has come from the personal experiences of others. Some came from watching and observing two young people in my own household take totally different approaches to living on their own. Hopefully, it will make your journey more enjoyable by helping you avoid some of the uncomfortable or frustrating situations that have confronted others.

When to Leave

Is there any *best* time to leave? Or, for that matter, is there a best time to arrive wherever it is you're going? Other than avoiding major holiday weekends, obviously bad weather or times of emotional stress, there appears to be no best time.

As you consider *when* to leave, the *reason* you're leaving will help provide an answer. If it is to accept a job, the starting date of employment will dictate when to pack up and take off. But even then, it is important to plan ahead.

If you're leaving because you've finished a semester of school or graduated, perhaps you'll want to weigh the pros and cons of moving on after a brief visit at home—long enough to gather up some needed belongings and supplies and say necessary good-byes. Leaving at the end of one last summer of freedom may have some appeal. Perhaps the answer is working at a summer job until the fall cycle begins, and it is time to get down to business.

When to leave also may be dictated by finances. You will need a certain amount of money to get started. Once you know how much, you'll have to withdraw the money from savings, borrow it from family or friends or earn it. Perhaps some of each. Regardless of where the money originates, you should know how long it will take to accumulate it and include that in determining when you will leave.

Once you've made up your mind, go! It will be easy to find excuses to stick around just a bit longer. And the longer you postpone the actual move, the tougher it will be for all concerned.

So, whether you are leaving home to establish your independence, to take a job elsewhere or because living at home is cramping your style, first set a timetable.

The Importance of Planning Ahead

Plan around a timetable but allow yourself ample time. Learn from the experiences of others and avoid mistakes that can be both costly and irritating.

Certain prior considerations are important. First, what resources are available? Where can you obtain information about your new community? Where can you get a map? Can your employer help in this respect?

Second, do you want to live in the city or in the suburbs? What kind of lifestyle suits you best? Learn the pros and cons of each. Think about your likes and dislikes, hobbies and recreational interests. Where can you find them, city or suburb?

Third, consider your *needs* versus *wants*. What you want may be impractical on your budget. What you need, at least initially, may be much more realistic. But check out the options ahead of time. Find out the cost of certain necessities before you move. Look into rent, utilities, deposits on utilities, initial outlay for work clothing, car payments, entertainment, food. While the total may be a shock, it's better that it comes when you're in the planning stage rather than once you've arrived.

Don't limit your options by rushing into anything. Take time to look around, read leases, canvass neighborhoods and to carefully check out factors that are important to everyday living.

If you have a job waiting, you're ahead of the game. The main task will be finding living quarters. You might want to talk with your employer about this. Some companies maintain a list of rental units that have been used by other employees or a list of employees who are willing to consider an apartment-sharing arrangement.

If you are looking for a job as well, you'll need more time, and living quarters probably should be temporary. Avoid long-term leases until you find the job you want. Either way, keep your living situation flexible.

Use Available Resources

Newspapers.   If you are "movin' on out" to a town or city that isn't familiar or where you don't know anyone, get a copy of the local newspaper, especially the Saturday or Sunday editions. There is no better way to get acquainted with a new hometown than through the paper—short of actually being there. The name and address of the daily or weekly papers serving the area to which you will be moving can be found by checking the *Ayer Directory of Publications* at your local library. The newspaper will be happy to mail a sample copy, and you can subscribe to the Sunday edition for several months for just a few dollars.

The newspaper will include a great many things about your new community—activities of general interest, theater or musical performances, events at local colleges and universities, sporting attractions, festivals and, most important, real estate rental opportunities, often with comparative costs. Start clipping the paper and build a research file for future reference.

Libraries.   If there is an opportunity to visit your new community, stop in at the library. Not only will you find copies of local newpapers, you also will be able to explore needs and interests with a librarian. It's amazing how much information is available. This way you'll feel more confident and in control once you arrive.

Maps.   It is worthwhile getting a local map right away. In larger communities, maps can be obtained from a variety of sources. Gasoline service stations often have maps at a slight cost. Book stores, gift shops and convenience stores frequently offer local area maps. If you are moving to a different state, visitor information centers lie just beyond the state line on many major highways. Most major cities have visitor information centers, too. Maps and other localized information usually are free for the asking.

In smaller cities and towns, real estate firms and banks often provide the same kind of information. More and more chambers of commerce in cities of 30,000 to 100,000 are producing printed "quality of living" booklets, handsomely illustrated, with information on churches, schools, major employers, parks, recreation areas, libraries, museums, sports activities, colleges and universities. They generally are inexpensive and offer a good way to get to know about the area.

If you are moving to accept a job and your company is a major employer in the area, ask the personnel or human resources department for information on the community, including a local map.

Learning About Yourself

One of the most important aspects of "movin' on out" is finding out who and what you are. If you were a star athlete in school, unless you've signed a pro contract for big bucks, once you're out there on your own, few people care about past glories. You're starting all over again. Most people on their own for the first time experience periods of loneliness. It won't be unusual if you do, too. And you, like them, will soon get over it. But how it is handled initially will tell something about yourself.

New Experiences

Most people making a move of this nature will encounter a variety of new experiences. What will be familiar to some will be almost overwhelming to others.

This is a point in life to explore, test new options, try new things and grow in many ways. Try city living if you've lived in a small town. It can be exciting. If you have lived in one place, travel regularly.

Dining out, visiting a courtroom, attending the ballet, an opera or a big league hockey game are all part of opening up a whole new world.

You will have to find a new doctor (Chapter 9); may have need for an attorney (Chapter 9); will want to open a bank account and establish credit (Chapter 6). Some, living alone for the first time, will feel a need for someone to talk to (Chapter 9).

New surroundings and new time schedules will create different shopping habits (Chapter 5). For some, the level of lifestyle will be considerably less than before. Managing on your income may require living in a neighborhood you wouldn't have considered a few years ago (Chapter 1).

In many cities, the cost of parking a car in a public lot near work may be prohibitive. So, you'll learn to use the city's public transit system.

There will be no one to pick up after you and do laundry. Food shopping, dry cleaning, shoe repairs, auto repairs, getting a local driver's license will have to be handled outside working hours. Buttons that fall off and seams that rip may present problems. Where can such things be repaired and at what cost (Chapter 5)?

Some of you will have initial experiences with insurance (Chapter 7). The insurance business is a maze few people understand, and the options for any kind of insurance—life, health and accident, automobile, tenant's or liability—are many.

Many of you will be buying household furnishings for the first time, largely on instinct, with little information about what, how, where and when to buy (Chapter 2).

Entering into legal contracts—leasing an apartment, obtaining a credit card, buying a car on time, signing a service contract, getting married—will present new experiences, regardless of your educational level (Chapters 1, 5, and 6).

There will be disappointments and, thank goodness, many successes. Many of the latter will be small and seem large—your first independent venture on the New York subway or an initial plane trip, perhaps. Disappointments likely will seem monumental at the moment and small in retrospect.

The Financial Reality

The place where people are confronted with reality almost daily is in the pocketbook. Whether you are employed in a trade, craft, service, profession or just looking for a job, the simple cost of living can be a rude awakening for the individual stepping out on his or her own.

"I've got a job. I'm earning good money. I have only myself to support." Familiar refrains, but often only barely connected with reality. The simple fact is that most people leave home with only the vaguest notion of how to get along financially. Discussions with parents on how to budget and the difference between fixed and variable expenses too often don't take place (Chapter 4).

By planning, using some common sense and developing some consumer awareness, an individual on his or her own can stretch money beyond what most people think is possible. And there is no better time to start than right now, while spending, budgeting and saving habits are being formed.

Defining "On Your Own"

Some of the best advice given by people who have been living on their own for several years relates to using the experience of others as part of the learning process. "There is no need to reinvent the wheel," they say.

This doesn't mean doing something the same as someone else. Rather, it means evaluating another person's experiences before making a decision.

Being on your own, therefore, doesn't mean you have to do everything yourself, to meet every challenge alone, without benefit of counsel (Chapter 9). It simply means *you* control the decision-making process.

In this book, we are focusing primarily on some of the practical aspects of "movin' on out." We examine problems people encounter—for which they are generally unprepared—in setting up a first independent living situation. I have written this book primarily for people who are "movin' on out," with the hope that it eases the moving process, helps them avoid some needless errors, increases the joy of being on one's own and makes the transition more palatable, at least from the practical standpoint.

But I admit the book also has been written with parents in mind. For as each individual strikes out on his or her own, regardless of the motivation for the move, a parent or two is left behind. The move is more traumatic for some parents than for the person leaving. Parents wonder if they have provided sufficient preparation for the move—with gnawing doubts that they haven't. Parents often feel abandoned and rejected, no longer needed.

While the focus of this book admittedly is on facts and the practical aspects of leaving home, the final chapter deals with a number of social and psychological factors of importance to all family members.

Hopefully, this book will help you, your parents, relatives and friends to better understand the range of decisions you will have to make and experiences you will encounter. Hopefully, too, it will help make "movin' on out" a strong, positive transition to independent living.

1

Be It Ever So Humble

The day has come. You're on your way to begin the often arduous and challenging business of finding a place to live.

Armed with copies of the local newspaper, apartment locations of interest circled, checked or underlined, a map of the area in hand, the search begins in earnest.

Seven Helpful Tips for Finding a Place to Live

1. *Consider that the cost of housing should be approximately 25 percent of your take-home income.* Some financial advisors will suggest that 28 to 30 percent is a more realistic limit in today's market. In some communities, this will provide a clean, comfortable one-bedroom apartment. In some large cities, New York, Los Angeles, and Washington, for instance, this percentage will be inadequate. You may have to consider commuting or sharing an apartment to accommodate your budget. Keep in mind that rents generally are lower in areas of high vacancy rate—run-down neighborhoods, less desirable locations, loca-

tions where an industry has closed down and people have left the area—than in highly desirable locales. In the end, it is you who will have to decide.

Following are average monthly rental figures for an unfurnished, two bedroom, one- or one-and-a-half-bath apartment incorporating 850 to 950 square feet of space. Rents include stove and refrigerator and all utilities except water. Figures have been provided by the American Chamber of Commerce Researchers Association, from its "Inter City Cost of Living Index," fourth quarter, 1983. According to this source, apartments are located in a middle management neighborhood. Rentals are subject to change and local rentals for cities not included here usually can be obtained from the local Chamber of Commerce.

Atlanta, GA	$387	San Diego, CA	$515
Charlotte, NC	$343	San Francisco, CA	$831
Denver, CO	$475	San Jose, CA	$567
Ft. Worth, TX	$414	St. Louis, MO	$327
Houston, TX	$370	St. Paul, MN	$380
Miami, FL	$468	Portland, OR	$322
New York, NY	$855	Seattle/Tacoma, WA	$406

2.*Before you start hunting, give a little thought to what you really need and want in an apartment.* If rock music is your thing and you expect to be playing the drums in a little group on weekends, you'll need a place to practice. Not all landlords will put up with this, and unless you're in the right living circumstance, you *and* your drums could end up on the street, quickly. If you are a photography buff and *must* have a darkroom, keep that in mind (an extra large bathroom might serve the purpose). If you lift weights, a basement apartment with a concrete floor will be more practical than the top floor.

In short, consider hobbies and avocations when looking for a place to live. It may take more time, but the quality of living will be better for it.

Apartments on higher floors, with a view, or those with patios or porches generally are more expensive than those without. An apartment at the end of the building, with windows on two sides, also is likely to cost extra. Such extras as swimming pools, game or meeting rooms, on-premise laundry facilities have to be paid for—and the tenants will be picking up the costs.

In other buildings, however, extras are just that—extra. You pay for the apartment alone and only pay extra for something you need or want.

3. *Take time.* Don't get forced into something less than desirable. Apartment hunting can be time consuming. Not only is someone in a new community exploring new terrain, and that takes time, but it sometimes is a month or more before an attractive apartment or living space becomes available. If a building has a number of uninhabited apartments and the landlord is anxious to have you move in, beware. Check around and find out why there is a high vacancy rate.

Time permits comparisons to be made. Compare neighborhoods, facilities and costs. It is difficult to do this with any certainty in an afternoon or even a weekend. Cost for the same amount of space, with identical facilities, can vary greatly between locations.

If possible, do your scouting several months ahead of the move.

Ginny R.: "I wish I'd started sooner. Because I waited until the last minute, I had to accept what I could get. All the places I was interested in had waiting lists or no openings. The place I took was a slum by my standards. Nevertheless, I didn't make the mistake twice. The next time, I started looking well in advance of my lease expiring."

Having some leeway and not being forced into making a decision also means it will be possible to plan ahead to accumulate funds for a security deposit and the first month's rent.

Tom T.: "When I moved to Milwaukee, I knew where I was going to be working, but that was about it. So, after checking rental ads in the newspaper, I took a single room in an interesting old Victorian house within walking distance of work. I rented by the week. This way, I only

needed a minimum of belongings, I wasn't locked into anything and I was able to save a little money for the first two
months. I spent a great deal of time talking to people at
work about the kind of places they lived in so I could make
some comparisons. I also used my evenings to drive around
and look at different areas and different living arrangements. It was time well spent. When I found something I
liked and could afford, I could move easily because I didn't
have a long-term lease and I knew what I was getting into."

4.*Use the phone.* To save valuable time, miles on the car, and
disappointment, use the phone. Make a list of questions unanswered by ads or simply things you need to know before inspect-
ing the place. (Does the rent include certain utilities, such as
heat? Are pets allowed, if that is important? Is there off-street
parking? etc.) Some living circumstances will be eliminated
quickly. Concentrate on other, more favorable, options. Then
schedule a time to inspect the apartment when someone will be
available to show you around and answer questions.

5.*Go alone.* Don't take along friends, pets or members of the
opposite sex, unless they remain in the car. They can and often
do distract from your primary purpose—to examine and compare potential living quarters. Real estate agents and landlords
want to be able to deal directly with the prospective tenant, and
extraneous elements can foul up things. If you've decided upon
an apartmentmate, however, it is appropriate to bring him or
her along.

If you are a woman and want the security and comfort of
having a man along while hunting for a place to live, remember,
you'll be on your own once appropriate living space has been
found. Don't consider locations where you are going to feel
uncomfortable.

6.*Schedule the visit at times when residents are in the building, if possible.* Around the dinner hour or Saturdays are generally good times. You'll get a better picture of the noise level in
the building when people are home. Inquire about the kind of
tenants living on either side and above the apartment being
considered. Sound in most buildings seems more pronounced
from above and the sides than from below.

After the inspection, consider returning at another time to talk to other tenants. If they are reluctant to talk to strangers or if there is a security system preventing access to them, there are at least two courses of action. First, wait in the lobby or outside the door for people to arrive, then introduce yourself and tell them what you are looking for. Second, if possible, take several names from the mailboxes, look them up in the phone book and call them.

7.*There are hidden, up-front costs that must be considered.* Most utility companies—gas, electric and phone—require a deposit before they will connect your service. These deposits can be substantial. The deposit is usually refundable after the tenant has moved out, unless you are staying in the area. In that case, the deposit stays with the company until the service is no longer needed. If you have established credit in the area, the deposit may be reduced or eliminated. Explore this with the utilities customer service representatives.

In some states, the deposit, by law, must generate interest. After all, the reasoning goes, if they are using your money, they should pay interest. It is worthwhile asking each utility whether the deposit (the legal term for keeping a deposit is "escrowing") will be earning interest for you while in escrow.

Often there is a fee for connecting a utility. This varies between cities, companies and even the circumstances of the user. Check it out so there are no unpleasant surprises.

Urban or Surburban Living

Another point to consider is whether you are more comfortable in an urban setting or if the suburbs have more appeal. Whether you are moving to Baton Rouge or New Orleans, Madison or Milwaukee, Lancaster or Philadelphia, Athens or Atlanta, Santa Barbara or Los Angeles, you still have the option of living in the city or the outskirts.

For people from small towns, the move is sometimes more comfortable if they stay in the suburbs. The change in lifestyle is less dramatic. Further, there are different resources available in the suburbs or smaller towns than in the city. Suburban newspa-

pers carry more detailed and localized rental advertising, and
often the variety in rentals is greater. Shopping centers generally have community bulletin boards on which apartment ads are
posted. Churches do the same.

Housing Options

If the job requires a great deal of travel or if you expect to be
away most weekends, a modest, one-room efficiency, more akin
to a hotel room, may do very well. If the conviviality of a roommate, yet some privacy, seems important, a two-bedroom unit
with living and dining space may be the answer. The options are
many and varied.

The Efficiency.   Generally the least costly, the efficiency is a
one-room, self-contained unit with a bath. In older units, a bed
sometimes folds up into what otherwise looks like a closet. Some
have a small, compact, combined cooking, sink and refrigerator
unit—designed to serve the modest needs of a single individual.
If you are active, out most of the time, and not interested in
entertaining at home, an efficiency may be your best bet. This
type of living arrangement doesn't offer any options for a change
of scenery, and the four walls may begin to close in at times.

Dave M.: "When I made my first move, I had a girlfriend
back home and planned to be there most weekends. Since I
don't—or didn't—cook, a kitchen wasn't important. I
wasn't home much in the early evening. Also, I expected to
be transferred at the end of a training period with the company. So, an efficiency seemed a good choice. Well, first, I
was assigned to the home office and not transferred. Then,
my girlfriend and I broke up. I found myself at home star-
ing at the walls on winter weekends. It became depressing.
I guess efficiencies have their place, but I'm planning to
move as soon as possible."

The Small, Converted Home Apartment.   Here the owner is
usually an individual rather than a corporate management company. This can be either a plus or minus. On the one hand, a

tenant may recieve better service when things need fixing. On the other, some degree of privacy may be lost with the landlord hovering around.

Some of these living arrangements are flexible and informal, and tenants usually get to know each other fairly quickly. If you are looking for an opportunity to meet neighbors, this often is a good way to do it. Such apartments often are more difficult to find and seldom have the conveniences or extras of modern multiunit complexes. They do have some charm and a lot of character. While they sometimes are advertised in local newspapers as openings occur, availability often is conveyed by word-of-mouth.

Try to identify older sections of the community with once stately homes. Drive through the area to see what it looks like, then start knocking on doors and asking about rental units. Some of these units can be rented on less than a full-year's lease. This offers an advantage at times.

Jack M.: "I knew I didn't want to live in an apartment complex. It was too close to dorm living. I wanted something warmer, more homey, perhaps with a little character. Well, I had gone to school here and I asked some of the faculty and administration people if they knew of any section of town where I might find what I wanted. They recommended the area I'm now living in. There are six apartments in this old house, and I know all the tenants. I have to go up three flights of stairs with no elevator, and that's inconvenient at times, but I know I made the right choice."

Multiunit Apartment Buildings. The most common and obvious rental unit is the large apartment complex. Every city has numerous such complexes, with varying degrees of appeal and in locations that should suit anyone.

Here are found newer, more modern units, generally with fairly contemporary utilities, laundry washers and dryers in the building, if not in the apartment, and, in some areas, ample off-street parking. It also generally takes more time and effort to get repairs made and to get a response from the management to any need. The place usually is run on a purely businesslike basis. This generally is the least personal type of living unit, and even after a full year, you still may not know the neighbors. It affords maximum privacy, despite the number of people.

> *Steve S.:* "People in my building keep to themselves. There is a guy down the hall about my age, and I've tried to strike up a conversation with him, but he doesn't seem responsive. Since I live alone, I have no one to talk to. So I'm thinking of getting a roommate."

An advantage of multiunit apartments is that they are numerous and thus easy to find. In most cities and towns, there are some high-rise units in the center of the city—usually expensive—and many low-rise—two to five stories—units in the suburbs. Many of the latter are near shopping centers for the convenience of residents.

A note of warning regarding rental apartments in large complexes. In recent years, there has been a significant move to convert apartment buildings to condominiums. Generally, these are more expensive facilities closer to the heart of the city, but any apartment complex is potentially convertible, and the number of apartments available in large buildings is being reduced sharply in many areas of the country. Since 1970, almost 400,000 rental units went condo, and the number of conversions is expected to rise to 1.1 million by 1985.

A House.   Not uncommon, but often overlooked, is the prospect of sharing a house. In larger cities, this could be all male, all female or mixed. In this type of arrangement, you'll immediately have a network of contacts with other people your own age or general background.

One of the major advantages of sharing a house is the cost factor. In Washington, for instance, seldom does an individual on his or her own for the first time earn enough money to immediately afford an attractive one-bedroom apartment in a pleasant location. So, many people share housing and split the cost two, three or four ways. Food costs, too, can be divided and similar savings effected.

Prospective housemates often are required to pass an interview with the other residents to see if interests and personalities are compatible.

Jim J.: "When I moved to Chicago, I knew a fellow who had been living with three other guys in a townhouse along the lake. Across the patio were two other townhouses with four or five guys each. My friend let me know that one group had an opening about the time I needed a place. They were all young business or professional types, and I passed the interview. They had the place nicely furnished and obviously were proud of what they had. I was asked to 'buy in' at what amounted to three months rent. This meant that I had a one-quarter 'ownership.' When I wanted to leave, it was my responsibility to 'sell' my one-quarter share to the next guy coming in. I thought it was a pretty good deal. It kept out the deadbeats anyway."

Building Security

Check it out before you sign a lease. Is the front door to the building locked at all times? Do individual floors have fire doors locked from the outside? Is there unsecured entry from the roof? Is there an audio system that allows you to identify visitors? Is there a security guard in the lobby? What kind of locks are on the apartment door? If the apartment is situated on the ground level, below ground level or first floor, are sliding glass doors and windows secure? Thieves will get into even the most secure buildings if they want to, but there is no sense inviting them by lax security measures.

Steve S.: "After I moved into my apartment, I found that everyone on the first floor had been robbed within the past year. Everyone! Being on the third floor made me feel a little more secure, but not much. Not that I had much of value, but what I did possess would be hard to replace. On several occasions, I locked myself out of the apartment. It was then that I discovered how easy it is to get into a locked apartment in my building. The landlord—actually the building management—said the construction of the building wouldn't allow a heavy dead-bolt lock. That was when I decided to move when my lease was up."

Maintenance

Talk to other tenants about the service and the service staff. If they characterize the building management people as sloppy and irresponsible or noncaring, that attitude may prevail when something needs fixing.

Disposal of garbage and trash can be an important factor. Try to find an apartment at the opposite end of the building from where trash and garbage are deposited. Trash and garbage attract bugs and cause odors, especially in warm weather.

Carole M.: "Early in my working life, I lived with a friend in a nice three-story building in suburban Washington. It had a pool, pleasant landscaping and, much to my horror, cockroaches! One of the problems, I'm sure, was the fact that the incinerator chute was just down the hall from my apartment. People threw garbage down the chute, and the bugs seemed to congregate in my end of the building. I called the management. They scheduled a pest removal company, which did some spraying. But it didn't do any good. In a few days, the cockroaches were back again. The next time, I sent a plastic package of cockroaches to the owner of the building by registered mail and threatened to go to a consumer protection agency if I didn't get results. The final answer was to move us to the other end of the building and to fumigate the entire apartment with every drawer, closet and cupboard empty. It was an awful experience."

The Lease: Read It Carefully

A FEW WORDS ABOUT LEASES

In virtually every living circumstance, you will have to sign leases before moving in. It will pay to: 1. Read the lease; 2. Ask questions; 3. Negotiate any important exceptions; 4. Delete anything you can't live with; 5. Keep a copy of the lease, *signed by the management of the building*.

The lease is written with the landlord's interests and rights in mind, not yours. But it can be changed or modified *if he or she is agreeable* and if it is done *before the lease is signed*.

Jack M.: "I read my lease and was concerned about all kinds of things, like 'no painting of walls, no nails in the walls, etc.' It sounded as if I couldn't do anything to decorate. So I talked to the landlord, told him what I had in mind and he said OK to the changes. It turned out he didn't object to changes as long as they improved the place and were done in good taste. The clause in the lease was designed to give him the right to evict someone if they made changes that were detrimental and might be costly to repair. If you are on good terms with the landlord or building management and are willing to make the changes yourself, at your cost, and in good taste, there is generally room to negotiate. However, I'd put it in the lease and have it signed. The guy could get fired or leave after agreeing to your requests, and if it isn't in writing, you have no protection."

Leases differ from building to building, city to city and state to state. Some states have uniform leasing laws that help protect the individual renter. (Consumers Union publishes a *Guide for Renters* for $1. It can be obtained by writing: Consumers Union, Reprint Department, Orangeburg, NY 10962.)

The local or state consumer protection bureau can offer renters' advice as well. More localized, most cities of any size have a housing agency that will be able to provide some guidelines on leasing and renting.

Some leases give the building management the right to enter your apartment at any time. If you have reason to disagree, read the lease and make sure it either isn't included or that it is removed before you sign it.

Likewise, some leases will require improvements to be left when a tenant moves, regardless of the investment. If you added mirrors, a special lock, overhead light fixtures or attached wall shelving added, prepare to leave it or fight with the landlord. If it's removed, the management will keep the security deposit, claiming it will cost at least that much to repair and repaint the areas involved. The same holds true for wallpaper and unusual paint colors on walls or woodwork. What one person thinks is terrific, the next may reject as hideous. The landlord benefits from neutral colors and no wallpaper in preparing the apartment for the next tenant.

When signing a lease for an apartment, make roommates equally responsible. Also find out from the landlord what happens if a roomie leaves. Get it in writing!

If you signed the original lease and are adding a roommate at a later date, get his or her name on the lease at that time. This assigns joint responsibility. *Check with the landlord at the time the apartment is taken to see whether the rent increases if a second or third person is added.* If it does, make certain the extra cost is borne by the roommate and make it absolutely clear what the rental fee will be for each person.

BREAKING A LEASE

Is there any legal way to get out of a lease? Yes, if the landlord breaks his obligation, as defined by the lease—if he fails to provide clean, safe premises, for instance. However, you may have to take the matter to court; few landlords will volunteer this. What is clean and safe to you may differ from what he considers to be clean and safe. The landlord knows that few tenants will spend the money or time to take a claim to court.

There is another avenue for leaving before your lease has run its course. It is not recommended, but it has been employed successfully more than once. Simply leave a month or two before the lease expires. Pack up and get out. Most landlords will not make the effort to track you down. They'll just keep your deposit fee and get the apartment back on the market as fast as they can.

Linda M.: "I planned to move when my lease expired. Thirty days prior to that point, I went to the office to notify them and found out that the lease required ninety days' written notice. The penalty I would have to pay to leave at that point would be payment of three months' rent with my written notice. And that was three months from the regular expiration date. On top of that, the management said they would keep my deposit until after I left to assess what damages were done and what repairs were needed. The total amounted to $1,200. I eventually solved the problem by subletting, but not before venting a lot of anger and frustration. And I could have avoided the whole problem if I had read the lease."

Some lease arrangements run for six months or a year and can then be renewed on a month-to-month basis. It clearly pays to check this aspect of the lease.

On occasion, if you explain that you have no choice in leaving—it is a requirement of the job or you've lost the job—a sympathetic and understanding landlord will release an obligation, usually for a partial payment.

One last point about apartment leases. *Don't assume anything about renewals.* Some leases are automatically renewable for another year. Some require notice from you, in writing, anywhere from thirty to ninety days prior to expiration, if you don't wish to renew the lease. While this fact may not seem important when you've found the ideal apartment and are anxious to move in, it can be very important and very costly when moving out.

SUBLETTING

Check to see what the lease says about subletting. This generally is the only legal recourse if you want or have to leave the apartment. Many apartments can be sublet (that is, rented to someone else), but the building management will want to investigate the prospective tenant in the same manner as he checked on you. And remember, the lease is in your name. If the person subletting skips out or does damage, you are the person liable. Subletting does not relieve the legal obligation incurred when the lease was signed. It simply means someone else has agreed to live there and pick up the monthly rental.

Rent Increases

As sure as the sun rises and sets, there will be a rent increase at some point. Some leases will have an automatic rental increase clause built in. Be aware of this and the history of rental increases in your unit. Most important, be prepared. Don't allow a rental increase to price you out of an apartment. The Consumer Price Index for Residential Rents rose substantially between 1975–1982. In New York City, it rose 50 percent. In San Diego, the increase was 80 percent, and in Cincinnati, 57 percent. The national average was 8 percent per year over the seven-year period. These increases usually come about on the anniversary date of the lease, but not always. Determine if the landlord is required to provide thirty, sixty or ninety days' written notice prior to an increase. The lease should spell this out.

Tenants' Associations

In recent years, especially in larger cities, tenants' associations have been formed to bargain collectively for tenants' rights. Legislation has been passed in many areas to help protect the rights of tenants. At the same time, landlords have joined together to keep track of bad credit risks and "troublemakers." These can range from people who physically tear up an apartment to known criminals to organizers for tenants' rights and individuals who take their unanswered gripes to the news media. If you're identified by a landlords' association as part of this group, be prepared. On the other hand, if help is needed in dealing with a balky landlord, consider joining a tenants' association, if there is one.

Following is a helpful checklist to assist in finding and obtaining a place to live.

A CHECKLIST

1. Have I budgeted adequately for housing?
2. Does the rent include utilities?
3. What kind of deposits are required for utilities?
4. Can I get any of it waived or reduced?
5. Will my utility deposits earn interest?
6. When will my deposits be returned?
7. Do I pay extra for parking, storage, use of a pool, etc.?
8. Can I reduce the rent by taking an apartment with a less desirable location in the building?
9. Can I save on rent and furnishings by sharing an apartment?
10. Where will I be able to park?
11. Is there adequate public transportation nearby?
12. Does my building or apartment have a place to do laundry?
13. Am I close to a convenience store, a supermarket, a drugstore, a cleaner?
14. Is the building management on the premises?
15. Is the neighborhood safe?
16. Is the building secure?
17. Is the building noisy?
18. Do I thoroughly understand my obligations in the lease?
19. May I decorate the apartment without violating the lease?
20. May someone stay with me temporarily without violating the lease?
21. May I sublet?
22. How much notice must I be given prior to a rent increase?
23. How much notice must I give prior to leaving?
24. Is my lease automatically renewable?

2

Movin' On In

OK, you've put down the deposit, paid the first month's rent, signed the lease and have a moving date. Now what? Well, now the fun begins, and you have a lot of work ahead.

Steve R.: "My first search for a place to live was complicated by the fact that I had a dog. Most apartment buildings don't allow animals. So, I found a lead through the local Community Opportunity Center. The apartment building was kind of ramshackle, but there were people living on the first floor. The owner was renovating upstairs. This was early in the summer. The owner said he would have the upstairs ready by the end of the summer, when I wanted to move. Well, I called the guy about two weeks before I was scheduled to move, and he said everything was OK. So, I packed up, and my folks and I arrived at the house to find nothing had been done. Nothing! There wasn't even any glass in the windows. Fortunately I hadn't signed a lease or put down a deposit, so I wasn't going to lose anything or have to fight to get my money returned. I finally found the owner, and he agreed to put me and my parents up at a local hotel for several days until I could find someplace else. I never want to go through that kind of experience again."

Making the Move

Begin by taking stock. What belongings and furniture do you own that you want to take? This will be determined somewhat by how far you're going and the practicality of moving large items. If you are lucky enough to be working for a company that is willing to pay for transporting your belongings, then by all means take everything you'll need or want, as long as there is adequate space.

HIRING A PROFESSIONAL MOVER

Most people will be solely responsible for moving their belongings on the initial move. There are several options available. First is to hire a moving company. This is the easy, though often expensive, way. Call several movers, ask them to inspect your belongings and estimate what it will cost to transport them between cities. Since the amount of your belongings is likely to be small, the mover will probably send your things along with someone else's shipment going to the same general destination.

Moving companies are loath to provide average costs for someone with a minimum of belongings. However, one reputable company noted that an *approximate* figure would be from $600 to $900 per 3,000 pounds. The mover took great pains to point out that several variables effect the final cost; the distance the apartment or home is from the truck, the number of flights of stairs, availability of an elevator, labor markets in various cities, and any special problems. It is more expensive moving into larger cities. The moving business is highly competitive; shop around and compare movers and prices before making a choice. Further, get an estimate in writing from the mover before signing a contract.

Professional movers will either pack for you or take your goods already packed. They will give advice on how to pack and can provide boxes, barrels and wardrobes for belongings; these latter at a cost, of course.

Professional moving companies are regulated by the Interstate Commerce Commission and have to follow strict rules. Most good movers will provide a booklet put out by the Commission called, *Your Rights and Responsibilities When You Move*, which explains what to expect. For instance, the mover has several days' leeway in delivery. You may sit in an empty flat waiting, painting, supervising phone installation, etc., while the moving company does its thing. *The mover also will have to be paid in cash, by certified check or money order*. Few will accept personal checks.

MOVE YOURSELF

Option two is to move yourself. If you aren't going too far (and you'll have to determine what is meant by this), try to enlist the help of relatives, friends or some high school kids who want to earn a little money. Beware: you must be specific about how things should be done and the timetable involved. Well-meaning people can turn the move into a party, and you could be left with a big mess and perhaps some damages. Friends also have no obligation to be reliable. Promises can be broken and people can fail to show up at the last minute. However, if your friends are reliable and trustworthy and packing and moving is done according to your schedule, it probably can be done for less money than the pros would charge.

In any move, schedule the activities well in advance. Check on rental vehicles unless a suitable truck is available. Most truck rental places have their equipment reserved several weeks ahead of time, so don't get caught short by calling on Wednesday to reserve a truck for Saturday. You may get a truck, but it may be the wrong size or a stick shift when what is needed is an automatic.

Consult with the rental company about the correct-size truck. They'll generally be able to tell from experience whether a truck is right for your needs. It's better to pay a bit more and have room left over than to have too little space and have to make two trips or leave something important behind.

The rental agencies also will have hand trucks to help move heavy objects, padding to protect furniture, should it be needed, and other equipment to help ease the strain of the move.

Renting a truck is like renting a car. Options differ. Some companies will charge a flat fee, and you pay for gas. Some will charge mileage and a fee and reimburse the gas costs. The rental agency will want to know that you are of legal age and have a valid driver's license. They will ask for the payment of insurance on the vehicle, as well as liability insurance, or for a waiver to be signed for both. If personal automobile insurance covers you in another person's vehicle, including a rental truck, the renter's insurance may not be necessary. Check with your insurance representative to see if you're protected.

If renting a trailer is necessary, make certain the trailer hitch will fit on the back of the car and that the car has enough horse-power to pull a full trailer without damaging the car. The rental company should be able to supply answers to these questions.

Find out ahead of time what costs will be incurred. I priced rentals at a major truck and trailer rental company recently and found that a small, 4 × 8 foot trailer can be obtained for $25 per day, plus $1.50 insurance. A 6 × 12 foot trailer is $35 per day, plus $1.50 for insurance. A 7-foot truck rents for $25 per day plus 25¢ per mile. Insurance is $6 per day, and the company requires $100 as a deposit. They accept major credit cards for the deposit. There is a hefty extra charge if you wish to leave the truck or trailer in the city of destination, and that varies consid-erably, depending upon the distance and location.

PACKING

If you are moving yourself, pack all belongings carefully and put them in one place. Label each box or bag. Don't leave anything for moving day, you'll be busy enough then.

Prepare for packing by gathering boxes from the grocery,

drug or liquor store. Also save newspapers. Boxes can be purchased from a professional mover, but throwaways from the stores should suffice. One exception might be a wardrobe or hanger carton for clothing to be kept on hangers.

If boxes are purchased from the moving company and you do the packing, the boxes will cost approximately the following:

```
Mattress box, single............................$4.60
Mattress box, double.............................5.40
Picture carton ..................................6.80
Lamp carton .....................................2.60
Book carton, 12″ × 12″ × 16″.....................1.75
Dish barrel .....................................8.40
Wardrobe, 23″ × 50″ × 24″........................6.65
Standard box, 22″ × 20″ × 23″....................3.65
```

In preparing to pack, carefully evaluate everything. Be tough in judging what to take along. Throw things out. Old clothing can be donated to the Salvation Army or local rescue mission. Books can be given to a library, school, hospital or local secondhand bookstore. A tax-deductible-contribution receipt, on which you establish the value of the items, can be gotten.

Wrap breakables in newspapers, item by item. Or make use of the towels and linens you are taking along by using them to wrap breakables. Books should go in smaller boxes, as they are heavy. Items such as coin collections, guns, silver, sensitive electronic gear and valuable papers should be kept with you rather than entrusted to the back of a truck, if at all possible.

You may decide not to take more than a few personal things, choosing instead to obtain furniture upon arrival. In that case, there are several other options.

Furnishing the Apartment

Renting or Leasing Furniture

An increasingly attractive option for many is renting or leasing furniture. There are well over 200 members of the Furniture

Rental Association of America scattered across the nation. A list of members of the association can be obtained by writing them at Suite 1325, 50 West Broad St., Columbus, OH 43215.

Whether your taste in furnishings is contemporary or traditional, they can help. These folks will rent a single piece around which to build a living room or they will furnish an entire apartment. Initially, renting is much cheaper than buying. And if there is some question as to how long you're going to be in the apartment, or city, for that matter, renting or leasing may be the best bet.

Costs can range from $12 to $30 a month for a sofa and $60 a month and up for a basic, sixteen-piece, two-room-apartment set. This is on a twelve-month lease. One can rent for as little as three months, but a premium is paid for that convenience.

Acquiring Furnishings Locally

When the costs of moving furniture from home or school to a new apartment are added up, it may make more sense to bring only necessary personal belongings and clothing and to acquire furniture locally. Fortunately, this can be done easily, relatively cheaply and entertainingly. It also is a good way to get to know parts of the community.

1. *Salvation Army, Goodwill and St. Vincent de Paul.* All three acquire old furniture and rebuild, clean or fix it. In some cases, they will replace torn or worn materials. While the furniture is unquestionably used, it is servicable and inexpensive. Across the country, local community service agencies provide this service under a variety of names. Inquire at your local library, at the citizen information number at city hall, at your church or synagogue or by checking the phone book.

2. *Secondhand Stores.* In Chicago, there are 132 listings for secondhand furniture stores. In Philadelphia, the number is 79, and in Phoenix, it's 81. The stores will range from clean and well run to filthy and cluttered. If you know what you are looking for, check out various items to see if they are

sound. Some of the best bargains may be found in a cluttered corner of a tiny secondhand store off the beaten track. Bargain with the owner. The merchandise seldom will be marked with a price, and the owner is likely to charge what he or she thinks you can afford.

3. *Discount Furniture and Department Stores.* This option begins to get into the more expensive choices. Discounters are likely to be less expensive than department stores, but not always. Be careful here. Just because a discounter says he is a discounter doesn't mean he offers every item at bargain prices. And the question is, "Discounted from what?"

Theory is that a discounter has deducted a certain percentage from the price one is likely to pay at a major furniture or department store. That may or may not be the case. Don't let yourself be talked into something. Check out any retail store, see what they charge for the same pieces covered with the same fabrics and then compare. And watch for sales. Some very good buys can be obtained on floor models that are available immediately. It may take eight to ten weeks to get an item if it is not in stock.

4. *Garage and Yard Sales.* Many communities, especially in the suburbs of larger cities and in smaller towns, have regular garage and yard sales. Here one is likely to find everything fron junk to gems. The secret is to get there early because the serious shoppers will be scouting the best buys before the sale begins.

Make a list of places to visit and know what you are looking for. Upon arrival, check out each place to see if they have it. If they don't, move on. The temptation will be to stay and browse. If the item is electric or mechanical, make sure it works before buying it. Don't take the owner's word alone. Further, if you can, determine why the owner is selling the stuff; perhaps they are moving, want to clean out the garage or just want to get rid of old junk. This will provide a better idea of what is likely to be available. On occasion, a phone number is included in the ad announcing yard and garage sales. The better items are usually listed, too. Get a local newspaper, not the major city paper, and canvass the classified ads. Yard and garage sales usually are held on Saturdays, and the ads often run in weekly papers on Wednesday evening or Thursday.

5. *Auctions*. Auctions are a specialty in themselves. Learn what occurs at an auction before attending one to avoid making mistakes. One excellent source of information is *How to Buy at Auction* by Michael DeForrest, published by Simon & Schuster. This simple, readable, 224-page book tells you virtually everything you'll need to know. Buying at an auction requires an early arrival to check out the merchandise, knowing your top bid and sticking to it. Be prepared to pay in cash and to take the item home.

6. *Unpainted Furniture Stores*. Here one gets what the sign says. The furniture is basic, simply assembled, adequate, functional, not particularly charming or imaginative. It needs to be painted. These items also are not generally bargains.

7. *Furniture Rental Resale Shops*. Bargains can be obtained from time to time. Rented furniture has been returned. Depending upon the way it has been treated or styled, it may be cleaned up and rerented or may be shipped to a resale store on some back street. On the right day, you may find something you like and can use, possibly at a big reduction.

8. *Thrift Shops*. These are usually run by a women's auxiliary of a hospital, church, synagogue or some other community service organization. The people who run them often do not have accurate judgment on what things are worth, particularly in home furnishings. Therefore, one can find some ridiculous prices. Many relatively well-to-do people seem to feel more comfortable donating things to this kind

of outlet. They get a tax deduction, something they wouldn't get if they sold their belongings to a secondhand store. Thrift shops usually are listed in the yellow pages of the phone book, often identified with the institution they are benefiting.

9. *Flea Markets.* Flea markets have degenerated a great deal in recent years and often are no more than displays for junk. Occasionally you'll find a true flea market where people have brought a variety of interesting goods, including some furniture. But I wouldn't concentrate on this option.

10. *Antique Stores and Marts.* There are antique stores and there are antique stores. Some are high quality, peddling real antiques, most of which will be out of your price range. They are fun to browse in, but they aren't going to solve your furnishing problems unless Uncle Harry has left some money you don't know what to do with. However, there are antique stores and marts in smaller, often rural, communities that can provide some bargains. Check classified ads. Inquire from friends and acquaintances in your new hometown. Perhaps they'll be able to steer you to one providing an interesting trip through the countryside and an enjoyable treasure hunt at the same time.

11. *Make Your Own.* This may sound ridiculous, but it isn't. It is amazing what can be done with a little ingenuity and some simple tools, wood and paint.

Coffee tables, end tables, lamps, bookcases, a bed and even what will pass for a sofa can be made with a few basic materials. A couple of foam pillows on a flush door with metal legs, placed against the wall with throw pillows, makes an inexpensive sofa and, in an emergency, a place for a friend to sleep for a night or two.

There are numerous books available from most bookstores or public libraries and articles in magazines, such as *Metropolitan Home, Handy Man* or *Popular Mechanics*, that can provide help in putting together simple furnishings.

FRIENDS AND FAMILY

While the most obvious source of furnishings is relatives and
friends, a few words of caution are in order. One young man I
know assumed that he would take his bed, his desk and bookcase
when he left home. His parents thought differently. He reasoned the items were his. They reasoned otherwise. They
weren't about to have an empty bedroom to furnish; if he was
now going to be on his own, they decided, he would have to
provide for his own needs. Not all parents and relatives take this
approach, but if the person moving is going to be truly independent, he or she shouldn't expect to have parental support that
includes furnishing part or all of an apartment.

However, it is more common for parents and relatives to help
the individual starting out as much as possible. One problem is
that the items they are willing to offer may not be wanted. Their
taste in decor may be different. Diplomatic ways may have to be
found of excluding that old rocking chair, the battered gateleg
table or the goldleaf glasstop coffee table from your furnishings.
But you may have to take the bad with the good as you start and
get rid of things later on.

THE BEDROOM

The most difficult thing for many of us to give up or do without is
a bed. Although I know people who have slept on the floor, in
sleeping bags or on makeshift sofas until they could locate a bed,
it is far better to bring one from home if possible. Whatever you
do, don't purchase a used mattress and box spring. You will want
to sleep well, so don't scrimp on bedding. Many stores will even
throw in a plain metal bed frame for free. If necessary, bed
frames can also be obtained new for less than $45 or they can be
purchased used from various sources for about half that cost.
Unless a fancy wooden bed frame is already available free, don't
waste initial furnishing dollars on the item. (For tips on buying
beds and bedding, see Chapter 5.)

In addition, and depending on preference and habits, you'll
need a desk or makeup table, perhaps a small nightstand and a
wardrobe or chest of drawers for clothing. If there is a lot of
clothing, two may be needed. Or leave some items at home until

they are needed or the seasons change. The last items you will need are blinds or curtains.

A rug for the bedroom is a good investment, although getting out of bed in the morning and hitting a cold floor will wake you up in a hurry. A simple, inexpensive rug will also add warmth to the room and may provide a basic color to use when decorating. Further, many apartment owners will require that 80 percent of the floor space be covered by rugs or carpeting.

Finally, lighting is something to look into. If you like to read in bed, a small table lamp or high-intensity lamp with a swivel neck on the nightstand will serve the purpose. A typical desk lamp will work on the desk or makeup table. If your bedroom has an overhead light, additional lighting may not be needed for a while, but chances are the area lighting arrangement will be much better. There also are many attractive wall lamps available at reasonable prices.

THE KITCHEN

Fortunately, kitchens are normally well-equipped, so many additional furnishings shouldn't be needed. If you have space, invest in a small "table for two." Kitchens never seem to have enough counter space, and a small table also provides a place for the toaster or toaster oven, napkins and bags when bringing in the groceries.

Beyond that, and a couple of functional chairs, other necessary items are those used for cooking, eating or cleaning. Start with a squeeze-mop. You'll also need a broom and a dustpan. Next are cleaning materials. A good all-purpose cleaner (liquid) for floors and walls, a powder cleaner for sinks and counter tops and an oven cleaner, if needed, will do for starters. Several sturdy sponges and at least one good-sized plastic bucket (large enough to get the mop head into) ought to put you in good shape. Oh yes, some paper towels will be a help. The cost for all these items is about $30.

BATHROOM

Bathroom decor is very personal. To some, the bathroom is a functional area. Beyond a couple of towels and a washcloth, toilet paper, soap and personal toiletries, it simply is a place to get into and out of. Decor is sparce. Others like to make the room cheery, with small rugs or even inexpensive carpeting, a plant or two, a cloth cover for the toilet seat, fancy shower curtains, matching or complementary window curtains (if you have a window) and a container for facial tissue. A small shelf unit to hold decorative as well as functional items might add to the charm. Of course, none of these items is vital, but for a lived-in, warm and comfortable look, you may want to give it a special touch or two. It is the first place most people encounter in the morning, and visitors likely will avail themselves of your facility.

While you are purchasing cleaning items for the kitchen, throw in the following for the bath: a toilet brush, sponge, some powdered cleanser, several bars of hand and bath soap, four rolls of toilet paper (it's cheaper in packs of four), a small brush and some tile cleaner, if you have ceramic tile. This should cost you from *$12* to *$15*.

If you have a shower, you'll need a shower curtain liner immediately. Later on you may want to purchase a shower curtain, but for now the basic plastic liner will suffice. You should be able to purchase one for $3.50 to $5. Buy a liner with magnets in the bottom so that it doesn't swirl around once the air starts moving when the shower is on. The magnets will hold the liner firmly against the tub.

And finally, if there is a window, you'll need curtains or blinds soon. The window will steam up when showering, but there may be times when you don't want the whole world watching you. In an old building, the window may be opaque. Perhaps it has a frosted pane. That will solve the immediate problem, but there still ought to be something over the window at some point.

Living Room

The living room in most apartments is the focal point of activity. It is where people read, watch TV, converse with friends and in general spend the most time. It should be friendly and inviting. Chances are you won't begin by purchasing all new coordinated furniture out of *Architectural Digest* or *Better Homes and Gar-*

dens. The place is more likely to be a mix and match arrangement. And it can look perfectly charming.

Pick one item in the room and build around it. For example, a fireplace. If you have an interesting view, perhaps off a porch or patio, focus on that. A special piece of furniture, a large painting, photograph or poster can also serve as a focal point.

Two items you might wish to start with as strong elements in the room are a rug (unless it is carpeted) and a sofa (preferably one large enough to sleep on). If the room is carpeted in orange, it may be incompatible with a turquoise sofa or chair. So, consider what there is to work with when looking at apartments. The carpeting may seem like an asset at first glance, but make certain you're not going to hate the place every day because the assembled furniture clashes with it.

When buying a sofa, it may be wise to compromise on its style to obtain a suitable color that blends well. Or, if the sofa is a gift and there isn't anything that can be done about it, consider covering it with a large bedspread.

Don't get carried away with painting the walls dramatic colors until pondering the consequences. Dark colors make a room look smaller. They are also difficult to cover when leaving. You are likely to lose your deposit because of the extra effort needed when repainting the walls. Stick with neutral shades.

Besides the sofa, other items for the living room should include at least three chairs, one of which may be upholstered; a desk, if there isn't one in the bedroom; a coffee table, which can be improvised from a number of things; a floor lamp; a small table lamp for the desk; an end table and bookshelves.

Bookshelves can be made from pieces of plain 1 × 10 or 12-inch pine boards and bricks, tile, cinder blocks or drainage tile, which can be found at most lumber yards. You can also buy tracks to put on the wall and ready-made stained shelving with metal braces to hold it up. But this is expensive. It might be worth saving that purchase until you're more affluent.

Coffee tables can be old trunks, pine or cedar chests or a piece of plywood painted or covered with cloth, supported by a variety of objects. Magazines such as *Metropolitan Home* and *Better Homes and Gardens* have hundreds of ideas for this kind of thing. *Better Homes* has an issue each year in which they provide 100 decorating tips for under $100. My bet is that at least one and perhaps several ideas can be used or adapted to your own interests and budget.

Depending upon the kind of windows, what floor the apartment is on, dressing habits, etc., you may want to avoid putting up something around the windows for the time being. If the expanse is large and curtains or drapes must be provided, it will be costly. Blinds may be a quicker solution, but they aren't cheap either. Perhaps you'll be fortunate enough to find a place where the last tenant has left curtains or drapes. But don't count on it. If the windows are small, the concern will be lessened, and the expense less costly.

STORAGE

Many newer apartment buildings are constructed with the knowledge that tenants will want to store things. Therefore, many have storage lockers that may or may not be included in the rental cost of the apartment. They usually are small, but with some discipline you can survive. It is a good place for bicycles and surf boards in the winter and skis and other winter gear in the summer. Extra books may go there, but it probably will be damp, so find out in advance what can be stored without damage and what should be kept in the apartment.

Security of the storage place may also be a problem. Most storage units can be easily entered if anyone really wants to do so, even with the best of locks. So make certain the lock is good and that your things are insured.

Here's one storage trick you may want to consider. Take winter clothing to the cleaners in May, ask them to clean and store them until the fall. That way the potential problems of moths and storage can be avoided at the same time. There is no charge for the storage, but there will be a hefty fee for the cleaning. Clothing needs to be cleaned a couple of times a year anyway, so just save for that expenditure and pick up winter garments in the fall at two-week intervals.

Personal Security and Safety

In large cities, and even in their suburbs, burglaries are commonplace. While there is no certain way to protect yourself against loss of belongings, good insurance coverage (See Chapter 7), a survey of the building, investment in good locks, smoke detectors and a fire extinguisher will go a long way in avoiding possible losses.

Barbara M.: "Security to me was a second floor apartment, a $30 dead-bolt lock, a phone in my bedroom and a look of confidence."

What makes one person feel safe and secure may be inadequate for another. But security and safety of your person, money, car and apartment contents will be a paramount concern as you move out on your own.

The Building. Depending upon the degree of security desired, a number of things can be done to protect possessions. First, consider a building that has a good security system. This ranges from a guard at the door or a doorman to locks on the lobby door and on those from the lobby into other areas of the building to doors that require activation of an electronic device to let people in. *None is foolproof.* Consider an apartment on an upper floor but one not directly beneath the roof. It is harder to burglarize. Avoid porches and patios with large sliding glass doors and apartments near exits, particularly on the first or second floors.

Obtain a vocal dog (if the landlord will allow). Get a peephole if the door doesn't have it already.

Never let in anyone who you don't know or delivery or repair people you aren't expecting.

Locks. Probably the best security measure is to have several locks on the door, especially a dead-bolt lock. What makes a dead-bolt lock so much better than a conventional door lock is that it cannot be pried back, because it is not opened or closed with a spring. Further, a good dead-bolt lock is made of hardened steel, usually is larger and the bolt can only be moved by use of a key or hand action. The usual tools used to bypass conventional locks are useless on dead bolts. A good lock will cost in the neighborhood of $35. If it has to be installed by a service person, the cost will increase another $25 to $40. So try to get the owner or management of the building to do the job before hiring a professional.

Always remember, most standard door locks can be bypassed easily by even an amateur burglar. A plastic credit card, a couple of wires, a good bolt cutter and a screw diver can work wonders in just a couple of minutes.

Burglar Alarms. Another possible security and safety device is the portable burglar alarm. This unit slips over the inner door handle, and once the handle is tried or the door is moved, the alarm is activated. This creates a noise that will scare away most burglars. It can be purchased for $10 to $25.

More expensive electronic devices, running into hundreds of dollars, such as those found in single family homes, can be obtained to tie in with doors and windows. You'll have to be the judge as to whether you want to spend that kind of money. Seldom will a landlord absorb an expense of that magnitude.

Smoke Detectors. A smoke detector is an inexpensive "must" item in my book. In some communities, they are required by law. Easy to install, detectors operate by themselves, require virtually no care and could save your possessions and possibly your life. One brand of smoke detector even calls the fire department to tell them something is up. Prices for the standard models run from $15 on sale to $24 on the high side, and anyone can install one in minutes. Some insurance companies will give a reduction in tenant's insurance rates if a home or apartment has a smoke detector. Consider purchasing two, one for the hall near the kitchen and another for the bedroom.

Fire Extinguishers. Equally important, in my judgment, is a fire extinguisher. A home-sized extinguisher can be purchased for under $25. But be aware that there are several different types. The difference relates to the kind of fire being fought; electrical, gasoline or oil, wood, cloth or chemical. Extinguishers are rated A, B or C, depending upon their use against the elements generating the fire. I recommend an all purpose ABC extinguisher.

Be certain to read carefully the material with the extinguisher before buying it. If you are looking for an extinguisher to keep in your kitchen, make sure it can be used effectively in that area.

Moving Day: A Checklist

Before you leave the house for the last time, run down the following checklist.

1. Do I have my driver's license or someone to drive for me?
2. Do I have the keys to my new abode, or am I certain there will be someone there to let me in?
3. Have I enough money (or traveler's checks) to live on until my next paycheck?
4. Have I closed out my banking connections, including checking, and opened an account or accounts in my new community?
5. Have I sent change of address cards to the draft board, magazine publishers, friends, my school (if appropriate), the student loan people, etc.?
6. Have I arranged for any full- or part-time employers to send my W-2 federal withholding tax forms to my new address?
7. Have I arranged to care for any pets or plants I am not taking with me?
8. Have I picked up anything I had at the cleaners?
9. Have I had the car serviced for the trip?
10. Have I made hotel/motel arrangements if necessary?
11. Have I let someone know my itinerary and where I can be reached in an emergency?
12. Do I have a card or numbers from my medical coverage with me?
13. Have I packed all the things I'll need to have with me the first day I arrive?
14. Do I have all the personal records (birth certificate, passport, etc.) I'll need?

3

Shaping Up Your
Living Quarters

I don't know about you, but I *hate* to paint walls and woodwork. Perhaps it's because as an art and architecture major in college, I reasoned that painting should be confined to canvas and be *of* people, still life or scenery, not *on* walls and ceilings (unless of course, you were Michelangelo or da Vinci). Or perhaps it was because I never took the time nor had the interest to learn how to do it correctly.

But now that you're in *your* own home, you may want it to look as attractive and comfortable as possible. You're likely to be spending a lot of time there, so be happy with the surroundings.

Although furnishing an apartment to suit your tastes may prove costly and take several years to realize, painting or wall-papering can make a major difference immediately. Just be sure to learn something about those two tasks before attempting either. This chapter provides some helpful information and offers tips on simple home repairs.

A HOME TOOLBOX

Every residence ought to have an assortment of tools to take care of simple home repairs. Such a kit can be put together new for about $100. However, first try scrounging, then buy what you're missing.

Basic to any home toolbox are a hammer and a screwdriver. The hammer should be a good quality, one-piece, drop-forged, steel-claw hammer. I note one-piece because I am not in favor of the less expensive and less substantive wooden-handle version. The head sometimes breaks off from the handle. A good forged-steel hammer with a rubber-sheathed handle costs about $9.50. For lighter jobs, you may wish to purchase a tack hammer, at about $6.50. This little item often has a magnetized end to help set tacks and brads.

Screwdrivers come in several forms and sizes. There are standard screwdrivers, with a single squared-head blade, and a Phillips screwdriver, with a beveled X-shaped head. You can buy both in sizes from the tiny to the very large. Unless you are doing watch repairs on the side or want to fix eyeglasses, the tiny size is not very useful. I suggest a range of four: ⅛ inch, ¼ inch, 5/16 inch and ⅜ inch. For Phillips-head screws, get No. 1 and No. 2 size screwdrivers. These should take care of virtually every need. You can purchase a set that includes the above for less than $5.

Because some tasks take place in small, cramped areas, a good investment is a magnetized screwdriver or one that has a small clamp to hold the screw and the blade together. This will avoid the frustration of having the screw fall down into a crevice and getting lost. Each could run between $2 and $5.

A handy tool to have around is a spiral ratchet screwdriver. This clever item is built to accommodate a variety of standard and Phillips screwdriver tips and runs about $11. It also doubles as a simple drill, using interchangeable drill bits.

Consider the purchase of two kinds of wrenches. First is a standard, adjustable 10-inch wrench, which has no teeth. It can be used for nuts and bolts of all sizes and opens to 1 inch at the mouth. Cost: $5.95 to $9.49. Second is a gripping-type wrench. This has teeth and a pressure clamp that holds the grip firmly without slipping. It is also referred to as locking grip pliers. Cost: from $3.69 for a cheap, serviceable unit to $9.75 for a high-quality one.

A 6-foot retractable steel rule is another must item. These wind up like a spring and are self- contained in a small metal box. Cost: about $1.95. Consider also a folding, extension ruler, at $2.49 to $4.49. This is a sturdy device that unfolds to 6 or 7 feet and folds back to about 13 inches long and 4 inches wide.

Sandpaper in various grades will prove helpful at some point. Sheets can be purchased for about 45¢ each. Keep rough, medium and fine grain sandpaper on hand. A plastic block, for about $1.50, is used to hold the sandpaper when in use. The sandpaper can get hot, and it will be easier on your hands.

From time to time you will want to cut something with a saw. There is no substitute for a good 24- or 26-inch steel crosscut saw. This ideally should be an "eight-point" saw, meaning it has eight teeth to the inch. Be sure it is fastened to the handle by four or more bolts to assure sturdiness. Cost: $12.50 for a good model.

Another cutting item is a retractable utility knife, at $2.99. This is often used for carpet or linoleum. The blade slides back into the handle when not in use. A good utility scissors (about $8.95) should be in every tool kit for a variety of uses. Get one with an offset handle. It will be easier to use when cutting something on top of a table or on the floor.

A glass cutter, for about $1.75, will help make replacement of window or mirror glass a snap.

Two types of pliers should be in every home toolbox. A long-nose pliers, used to form terminal loops in electrical wires, to cut wires and for getting into hard-to-reach places runs about $5.60. A plastic-coated handle guards against shock in electrical work. The 7-inch version is about right for most uses. Second is a familiar item called a slip-joint pliers. This is what most of us think of when we say pliers. It is a multipurpose tool with a mouth that enlarges to accommodate various-sized objects. Great for gripping and bending, its sharp toothed jaws can leave marks on anything it is holding, however. Cost, $2.49 to $4.19.

A staple gun will come in handy. A heavy-duty model with attachments for fixing screens and tacking down electrical wiring costs about $20.

Three electrical items should be included. First is a flashlight.

This is a battery-powered item, rather than a plug in, but because it uses electrical energy produced by the battery, it's in this category. A good plastic or hard rubber model costs $4.25, with batteries. Next is a heavy-duty trouble light. This is great for working in dark places, such as under a sink. It has a wire mask-type device that protects the bulb from bumps and clanks and a hook so it can free your hands. It comes with a 25-foot cord and retails for $8.99. Third is a voltage tester. This simple little device, at $2.49, tells if electricity is on at a receptacle or a light fixture. It is truly shocking that so few people have one of these devices around the house.

While discussing household repair items, a word or so should be put in for safety gear. To protect eyes, lungs and hands, there are goggles, a respirator face mask and work gloves. While they add a total of $8.50 to the cost of the home repair kit, the safety aspect of having and using them can't be overstated.

There are many other items and an assortment of good power tools that could be included here, but at this stage we're talking about basics.

Planning Ahead

Plan ahead! Choosing colors or designs and then painting or papering is not something to rush into. Once it's done, you'll have to live with it.

Perhaps you will want to pick up a tone from the color of the furnishings in the room. If there are a lot of earth colors, for instance, you may want to make the walls a soft beige. If the room is dominated by a large dark blue sofa and you have drapes or curtains containing blue, a powder blue for the walls might be nice.

Check magazines or books with color photographs of rooms decorated professionally for ideas that might blend with or complement your belongings. Large posters or a wall hanging can also be used as a base for selecting colors.

Joe T., Paint and paper store manager: "When choosing paint colors, remember that you probably are picking the color in a store under fluorescent light. You should look at the color chip under the light you will have at home. You should also isolate the color chip you are interested in from the others. Some colors tend to change appearance next to other colors. In my experience, however, I find people get too wrapped up in splitting hairs about color, because the final result is usually OK, and it seldom matches exactly the way they envision it anyway."

Whatever your choice, unless you know exactly what you are doing, avoid strong, dark or bright colors. There are two reasons for this advice. First, if you are renting, the landlord may go bananas if he or she discovers the walls painted red, black or deep purple. It may seem dramatic to you, but to him it means extra work to cover it up later. Second, dark colors make a room appear smaller, and dark or bright colors tend to overwhelm everything else in the room.

Next, as part of your planning, be sure to have enough time to complete the job once it's started. It can be a terrible inconvenience to begin a job one weekend and finish it the next. If it is likely to take three days, work on it over a three-day weekend or take a vacation day and combine it with a standard weekend. Unless you are an experienced painter or paperer, count on the job taking more time than originally planned.

Also, make certain you have everything needed to do the job. There is a high level of frustration in painting or papering. Interrupting a job to go to the store or needing something at 10 P.M. Saturday evening when everything is closed can be more than frustrating; it can mean a botched job, frayed nerves and frazzled friendships.

Painting

What is needed depends somewhat on what is being painted, the kinds of paint to be used, how many people are helping and whether you are painting with the "quick and cheap" philosophy or taking the "beautiful and long lasting" approach.

WHAT IS NEEDED

Assuming you are doing nothing out of the ordinary and are painting one or two rooms and a bath in a standard apartment building, the following are likely to be needed: a roller, a roller frame, a paint pan and an extension pole that fits into the handle of the roller frame. Rollers come in different widths and with different nap thicknesses. The rougher the surface, the thicker the nap. For normal plasterboard drywall construction, a standard nap and the widest width roller should be used. A 2-inch roller will be helpful for smaller areas, such as the woodwork between doors, above windows, in corners, etc. The roller handle extension will help reach the tops of walls and the ceilings with ease. The approximate cost for the five items is in the range of $11. A plastic liner for the pan, which can be discarded after painting, runs about 50¢ and is worth it.

Purchase a putty knife ($3.50), an oval trim brush ($3.95), a 2-inch brush for trim, woodwork and windows ($2.50). Also get some petroleum jelly to protect glass areas from paint, perhaps a couple of single-edge razor blades ($1.50 for both) and a roll of masking tape. A small, 2-pound package of plaster, ready for mixing, costs about $1.20. Spackle will run about $2.50 a pint. Putty sells for approximately $1.60, and a tube of wood putty or plastic wood will cost in the neighborhood of $2.50 for 4 ounces.

There are several more items to go, so don't put the shopping list away yet. Unless you have a very sturdy and serviceable wooden chair, I'd suggest buying a small folding ladder. A 5-foot wooden ladder often can be obtained for less than $15, and you'll find many uses for it over the years. It is generally a good investment.

Next, for less than a dollar, is a plastic or cardboard paint pot. Painting out of the can is messy. Pour the paint from the can into a paint pot and then reseal the can. This way, the paint in the can won't form a rubbery layer on top, and the mess is lessened.

Paint thinner (at $2.45 a quart) is a necessity when using an oil-base paint on woodwork. Finally, buy some sandpaper; a couple of sheets if there is a lot of sanding to be done and two different grades—fine and medium—ought to work well. (Sandpaper is about 45¢ a sheet).

Total expenditure, before purchase of a drop cloth and paint, should run somewhere between $45 and $55.

The subject of drop cloths is one about which one can get into heated debate. Some people swear that it isn't needed; old newspapers make the most sense and are less expensive. It is true they are cheaper, but they can leave ink marks on floors, rugs and furniture, and unless applied in several layers, the paper doesn't prevent the paint from seeping through.

Others will say that a plastic drop cloth is best because the paint can't leak through, the material is cheap and it is not cumbersome to use. On the other hand, a canvas drop cloth will last a lifetime, provides the best protection and is used by the professionals.

Costs range from nothing for newspapers, to $6 to $8 for plastic, to $20 for a 9 × 12-foot quality canvas cloth. You'll have to make your own choice. On this we have no recommendation, although paint store managers recommend the canvas version, if you can afford it.

Understanding Paints

There are several facts to aware of before venturing into a paint store. For the kind of job you will be doing, there are basically two kinds of paint: latex and oil-base.

Latex-Base Paint. For walls and ceilings, consider a durable and easy to apply latex-base paint. This type is water soluble; it is, therefore, the easiest paint to clean off of brushes and rollers, hands, face, hair and clothing. Simply wash off paint with soap and water. Latex paint is sometimes referred to as water-base because of its water solubility.

Oil-Base Paint. This type of paint almost always is used for woodwork because woodwork gets dirtier easier, and woodwork covered with oil-base paint is easier to clean. Because of this and its durability, semigloss or full-gloss oil-base enamel paints are often recommended for the kitchen and bathroom areas. Both latex-base and oil-base paints come in three finishes: flat, semi-glossy and glossy. Obviously, this refers to the degree of shine. Enamel is a term the industry uses to describe the hardest finish of semigloss or glossy paints. It is available in latex- or oil-base paints. Except as noted above, walls seldom are glossy or semi-glossy. Woodwork may have either a partial or a strong shine to it.

If you have a wall that is wood-grain paneling, consult with the landlord before painting it. He/she may not want it painted. If it looks shabby and you want to improve its appearance, obtain and apply a penetrating seale or a stain; it will look 100 percent better.

Preparing Surfaces

This definitely is *not* the fun part of painting. More paint jobs are ruined because the surface has not been prepared correctly than for any other reason, according to painting experts. So don't overlook this step.

A *Home and Garden Bulletin* produced by the U.S. Department of Agriculture states, "Preparation of the surface—cleaning and patching—may take the most time in painting, because it is of major importance to the job. Even the best paint will not adhere to an excessively dirty or greasy surface or hide large cracks or scratches."

The surface to be painted should be clean, firm and smooth. All cracks and scratches should have been patched and sanded, nail holes filled and smoothed, to assure a successful paint job. Patching, using a quick-drying plaster, is required with significant holes or cracks. Spackle, a similar substance, is used to fill nail holes, small cracks and chips. Wood putty can be used to fill holes and cracks in wood finishes on door or window frames. If you are going to take the time and effort to paint, do it correctly.

Because of grease and moisture, kitchen and bathroom walls and ceilings usually need the most preliminary attention. The contents of aerosol cans too, get into the air and stick to walls and ceilings. Use a detergent, an ammoniated cleaner or a good all-purpose cleaner to do an effective job.

For living room and bedroom walls, a lot depends upon if you are a smoker (or your predecessor was) and whether you have a fireplace or forced air heat. All of these things leave a film on walls and ceilings that should be cleaned thoroughly before beginning to paint. The same holds true for woodwork.

If the apartment has new drywall construction and yours is the first paint to be applied or if walls have been badly soiled, discolored by the sun or heat, patched or are a dark color, a primer coat of paint will be needed. A primer prepares the wall for the main coat and negates the need to apply two coats of the more expensive paint.

There are several kinds of primer. If the wall is in pretty good shape, a latex primer may work. But if it is a rough surface, has had a lot of patching or you are switching from a dark to a light color, try an alkyd primer, costing about $11. Uncertain which to get? Read the manufacturers' directions and comments on the labels. If you're still unsure, talk to an experienced and reputable paint dealer.

Quantity and Cost of Paint

Paint cans usually provide information about the number of square feet the contents of the container covers. A gallon of paint probably will cover from 400 to 450 square feet, or an average 9×12-foot room. To figure out total square footage, first calculate ceiling square footage by multiplying the length of the room by the width. Next multiply the height of the room by the length of each wall. Add those figures together and subtract the area occupied by doors and windows and you will have the number of square feet to be painted. If you expect to apply two coats, multiply the square foot area by two.

Enamel covers about the same square footage per gallon as flat paint. Therefore, woodwork should only require a pint or two.

Latex-base paint costs about $12 to $15 a gallon for white or standard chart colors. Add another $3 to $5 per gallon for decorator colors and $1 to $2 more for special mixes. The cost can be as much as $20 a gallon at a quality paint store.

A cheaper quality paint can be purchased at a discount store. Or buy a store brand or wait for a name brand to go on sale. Paint for ceiling, walls and woodwork in a 9×12 foot room should cost about $25.

Why buy the more expensive paint products? For several reasons. First, as explained, you sacrifice special mixes and decorator colors when buying off the discount store shelf. Second, discount stores seldom have knowledgeable, service-oriented people with whom to consult. A store that specializes in paint usually employs an experienced salesperson who can share shortcuts or special knowledge. Third, with a paint store, you have dependability and reliability should there be problems. If you run into a problem while painting, the paint store people will be happy to provide advice. This isn't possible at most discount or department stores. If there is something wrong with the paint or the brush or roller, the paint store manager will stand behind the product.

The paint business, just like any other, is always developing new products and new techniques. Your store manager will know them. And he'll share them with you if you give him a chance. He'll help outfit you for that paint job without breaking your bank, will advise you to avoid something if he observes that you are headed in the wrong direction and will help you avoid costly or time-consuming mistakes.

LET'S PAINT

First, move all the furniture out of the room, if possible. If not, move it to one side and cover it. Lay the drop cloth or newspapers on the floor along the soon-to-be-painted wall. Remove or tape electrical outlets if you do not want them to be painted. Otherwise, paint over them, but be careful not to get paint into the openings of the outlets. It's better to paint these carefully with a small brush.

Before applying paint, thoroughly mix it with a wooden paddle. They are free at most paint stores. Next, read the labels and follow directions.

If you are using a roller, pour the paint into the pan. Move the roller back and forth until the nap is uniformly covered, connect the handle of the extension and you're ready.

Ceilings and Walls. Start the ceiling in one corner and make firm but easy strokes back and forth, overlapping each stroke. If you have missed an area or haven't covered it as well as you'd like, now is the time to go back over it.

If you are going to paint the walls the same color as the ceiling, don't worry if you get a little paint on the walls at the point where the ceiling and wall join. After you are several feet away from the wall, go back and carefully fill the area where the wall and ceiling join using either the small 2-inch roller or the oval brush. Repeat this with each adjoining wall.

If there is a ceiling light fixture, use masking tape around the base of the fixture or remove the fixture before painting.

Then start on a wall. If you are right-handed, begin in the upper left-hand corner and work out and down. Reverse the process if you are left-handed. Use the same procedure around door and window frames that you did at the joints of walls and ceiling. If you prefer to tape the wood, that's okay. If paint gets on electrical fixtures or woodwork, a damp cloth will take it off easily if done before it dries.

While painting the walls, and if room permits, continue using the long-handled roller, especially on the upper portions of the walls. *Do not stop in the middle of a wall.* If you let paint dry and then try to paint next to or over it, you are likely to leave streaks. Further, as the paint drys, it will look slightly different.

Periodically stir the paint; stir rather than shake. This is important to maintain the consistency of the color, particularly if the color had been custom mixed.

Woodwork.   To prepare woodwork, lightly sand the surface of the previously painted area. This way the paint will adhere better. However, wash the surface down well after sanding so a powdery residue doesn't contaminate the new paint.

Here you probably will be using semigloss or glossy enamel. Since you know the properties of latex-base paint, let's discuss use of oil-base on the woodwork.

For oil-base paint, substitute some paint thinner or turpentine for soap and water to clean drip spots. But be very careful not to drip or spill it on painted surfaces. Turpentine will damage the paint job already completed. If paint gets on window glass, after it has dried, use a razor blade to scrape it off. An option for avoiding the cleaning of paint on glass surfaces is to coat the part of the window near the woodwork with petroleum jelly.

Wallpapering

Wallpapering and painting are as different as night and day. While you can paint by yourself, wallpapering usually requires someone to help. You may need patience and understanding far beyond the norm, depending on your temperament.

> *Joe T., Paint and paper store manager:* "If you're renting and the landlord requires the apartment to be returned to the 'original' condition when you leave, you will have to remove any wallpaper you added and restore and repaint the walls. That can take a lot of time and money. All this must be considered in making a decision to paper."

Now, if you still want to try papering, here are some hints. Wallpaper is more durable than paint, can be more decorative, is easy to clean and doesn't pick up dirt like paint does. If applied properly, it will last ten years; in contrast, paint only lasts three to four years. Keep this in mind if you're not likely to stay that long at your present address.

Measured against these advantages are several disadvantages. First, wallpaper generally is more expensive. Second, it must be properly applied or seams will separate, patterns will not match, bubbles will appear and the overall appearance will not be what you envisioned. Finally, you *must* have an aptitude for this kind of activity. It requires manual dexterity.

Preparing the Surface

As in painting, preparing the surface before papering is of maximum importance. It should be clean and smooth. Most wallpaper specialists will advise you to "size," that is "seal," a wall surface before papering. A painted wall is not necessarily sealed.

Sizing comes in ready-mix acrylic or in powder form, to be mixed with water. The former costs in the vicinity of $10 per gallon and covers about 500 square feet. The latter is about $2, covering about 400 square feet.

If you have removed existing paper and the surface of the wall is rough or if paint begins to fleck off, sand the wall. Then dust or wipe it clean. Glossy surfaces should be sanded and any cracks repaired. If the walls have any mold on them, use something like Clorox to remove it and let it dry thoroughly before applying the paper.

TOOLS OF THE TRADE

A wallpapering tool kit with most of the necessary items will contain a brush for applying paste to the back of the paper, a brush for smoothing the paper once it is on the wall, a seam roller, a razor holder and blade for trimming and a cutting guide. A good kit will also carry a string and chalk with a plumb bob to help determine straight lines.

In addition, this activity requires a drop cloth (plastic will do in this case), a medium-sized sponge, a yardstick, some pencils, a plastic bucket, some towels and, if you have prepasted paper, a water tray for dipping the paper.

Two other items are important: the wooden ladder previously mentioned and a wallpaper table. The table usually can be rented from your paint and paper shop and often comes with an edge for trimming.

COSTS

Materials, excluding paper, should cost in the vicinity of $40, including rental of the table. Paper can range from the very inexpensive to the very expensive; under $10 for a cheap roll, $20 to $30 for a designer roll. You generally are safe at something in the middle. Plan on approximately twelve rolls for a 9 × 12-foot room.

When buying a number of rolls of paper, make certain they are all from the same dyelot number. Two different dyelots could produce a marked variance in the color tone or hue of the paper.

Be aware that some papers, though priced at the single roll cost, only come in two-roll packs or as double rolls. Know, too, that some rolls will have to be ordered. Find out the delivery time. If the paper is needed this weekend and you have found a delightful pattern, you may be disappointed if it takes two weeks to obtain.

Plan on a total expenditure of approximately $220 to paper a room, including all materials. It can be done for less if equipment is borrowed, you mix the paste and you use cheap wallpaper. Only you will know what you want, need and will be satisfied with.

If you think you may have overpurchased, you may be able to return the extra, unused roll. Check with the store manager for store policy. If possible, get an agreement from the store manager, *in writing*, before leaving the store.

KINDS OF PAPERS

There are many kinds of papers. The two basic types are prepasted, where you simply dip the paper in water and apply, and the nonpasted, where you mix and apply the paste to the paper before applying. Although it is more time consuming, for best results, I suggest the latter.

Beyond that, there are plain papers, papers with flocking or otherwise raised surfaces, vinyl papers for bathrooms and kitchens and papers for covering masonry or brick. Inquire about special needs, if you have them, with the paper store manager. Read the information contained in the books that display wallpaper samples. You can learn a lot and avoid costly mistakes. In fact, read directions on everything—on the tool kit, the paste can or mixture, even on the paper. And follow them.

TIMING

If you're fairly handy, work quickly, don't stop for breaks, have a friend to help and have prepared ahead of time, you should be able to do an entire 9 × 12-foot room in a day. This is assuming there aren't any tricky corners and there are only a few openings in the room, such as windows and doors. A good professional could probably do it in half the time, with half the bother. If you choose, the wallpaper store manager probably will recommend a reputable paperhanger. You may wish to get an estimate or two.

Fixing Things: Simple Home Repairs

Before signing a lease, make certain who is responsible for typical repairs. Will you have to find a plumber if a radiator pipe breaks or freezes, or will the landlord? What about the cost for a safe door lock? Are you responsible for the repairs on the stove, refrigerator and hot water heater, or will the building management take care of maintaining these items?

As an apartment dweller, you should be able to refer serious "fix it" problems to your landlord. And if they are reasonably efficient, the problem should be quickly resolved.

If repairs are simple and inexpensive, it may be easier and far less costly to try to do them yourself rather than taking the time to try to cajole the maintenance people or waiting until an outside repairman gets around to it. The following are some tasks that fall into the do-it-yourself category.

FUSES AND CIRCUIT BREAKERS

First, find out if you have a fuse box or a circuit breaker system and where it is located. If the apartment is relatively new and in an apartment complex, look for a metal box set in the wall in the back of a closet, under the sink, at the back of a cupboard, in the hall, near your washer and dryer, if you have one, or in a nearby utility room.

If the home is older, the fuse box or circuit breaker may be in the basement. Ask the landlord. And find out if the electrical system serves just your apartment and you are on a separate meter or if it serves the entire house and you are billed proportionately.

If there is a fuse box, determine what kind of fuses the box uses (probably some 20 amp and some 30 amp) and buy a small package of each kind. A package of five 20 amp fuses costs about

$1.50. Keep them near the box. If a fuse blows, the little glass window on top of the fuse will appear cloudy or blackened. It may be that a small metal piece inside the window has melted. In either case, turn off the main switch to disconnect the power, unscrew the fuse and replace it. It helps to keep a flashlight handy in your apartment for this kind of emergency.

If you have a circuit breaker system, the process is easier. There either will be a switch, in a different mode than the rest of the switches (like a light switch on the wall), or there will be a little window next to a button that says whether the circuit is on or off. Simply flip the switch or push the button to activate the circuit again. This should have been turned off.

If the fuse is replaced, the switch thrown or the button pushed and nothing happens (if a fuse box, remember to turn the main switch on again), call the landlord or maintenance man to take a look at it.

APPLIANCES

If an appliance fails, the most likely culprit is a faulty plug or cord. Both are simple to repair.

First, test the plug. Try prying the metal prongs slightly apart and fitting the plug into the receptacle again. Also try reversing the plug or inserting it into another receptacle. If none of these things work, replace the plug.

Unplug the cord from the wall and cut it just behind the plug head. Leave about one-half inch of cord attached to the plug. Then take the plug to a local hardware store and show it to the clerk. Ask for a replacement head. It is very likely that you will be able to obtain a two piece plastic plug for less than a dollar. Then, simply: (1) split the cord into the two separate wires, which are evident, (2) insert the wires into the plastic piece, (3) push the covered wires down over the metal prongs inside until they pierce the rubber covering, (4) snap on the second piece of plastic and you are in business.

In some older cords, you will find two insulated wires inside a single round cord. This requires a different kind of plug, usually round, with a cardboard cover over the wire terminals. They are priced at 15¢ each. In this case, each wire will be inserted through the hole in the back of the plug and wound clockwise around a terminal screw. Then tighten the screw. (About an inch of the rubber insulation on the wire may have to be clipped away to make the connection.) Slip the cardboard cover back on and plug it in. If you have any questions, ask at your hardware store. In either case, it is a simple and inexpensive procedure and one you should not hesitate to tackle on your own.

The second problem with appliances could be the cord. Examine the cord carefully and see if you can see or feel a break in the wiring. If so, the cord can be repaired almost as easily as the plug.

First, unplug the cord from the wall. Then cut the cord at the point of the break. Cut away enough wire to eliminate the break. Next, separate the two wires in each section of cord and peel away about an inch of the covering over the end of each wire. Twist the many tiny little wires in each section so they become one wire. Then wind the wire from one piece of the cord to the wire of the other. You should now have two pieces of wire connected to each other. Repeat the procedure with the remaining two sections of wire. Now wrap each set of interwined wires separately with electrician's tape. (You can get some at any hardware store for $1.50.) Once each is secure, wrap the two wires together with the tape. It'll be almost as good as new.

LAMPS, LIGHT SWITCHES AND RECEPTACLES

If a lamp doesn't work, check the bulb. Replace it if necessary, but make certain you don't put a 100 watt bulb in a light fixture that is only rated for 75 or 60 watts. Most light fixtures will have the maximum wattage allowed stamped into the metal bulb receptacle. If the lamp still doesn't work and the plug and cord have been checked, I suggest taking it to a repair shop unless you are very handy and know more about electrical appliances than I am prepared to discuss here.

If the light is a fixture connected to a wall switch or if you are having trouble with a receptacle, they are easy to replace.

Before you do anything, *make certain the power supply is*

disconnected. Remove the fuse if you have fuses or switch the power line off on the circuit breaker.

Begin by unscrewing the plate that holds the unit to the wall surface. It may be necessary to undo another set of screws that connect the unit to a metal box set into the wall. Then, pull the unit out of the wall so the wires leading to it can be seen.

Unscrew each terminal screw far enough to slip off the curled wire wrapped around it. Make sure you know exactly what kind of a unit you are replacing. Compare the old unit with a replacement at the hardware store. Some units will have two terminals and some three. The replacement must match the original unit.

Once you have purchased a new unit (cost: $1.29 for a wall switch, $1.10 for a receptacle), slip the wires back around the terminals in the same manner as they were removed, tighten the screws and replace the unit in the metal box. Then insert and tighten the next set of screws. Before replacing the plate or cover, turn on the electricity and flip the switch. If you have purchased an identical unit and have followed directions, the switch should work. Finally, replace the wall plate.

Follow the same directions for replacing a wall receptacle.

PLUMBING

Plumbing can be more complicated than electrical repairs. But there still are some simple problems that can be corrected without having to call for help.

One problem common to repairs of most things is that it is easy to get into the middle of the repair process and find a need for some relatively minor items from the hardware store. To avoid this, develop a detailed description of the problem and the plumbing unit you are working with. Discuss it with the hardware store person. If, for instance, the type of faucet you are planning to fix has a specific brand name (it should be imprinted on the faucet somewhere) and you can accurately describe it, you may be able to get exactly the item or items needed before beginning the repair job. It is always better to get too many parts and return them later than to have too few and have to go back to the store.

Before beginning any plumbing work, make certain you understand how the components fit together so they can be reassembled. One way to accomplish this is to lay each piece you remove down on a counter or floor *in the order in which it was removed.* That way the items will be replaced in reverse order, starting with the last item removed. Some people find it helpful to make a simple sketch of each item in the order in which it was removed. Most fix-it books will give you detailed drawings of the way something is put together.

Faucets. Probably the most common problem you will have is a leaky faucet. There are several kinds of faucets. I will deal with two of the most common. If the apartment has old-fashioned plumbing, you may have stem faucets. To fix a stem faucet, first turn off the water leading to it. If the faucet you are fixing is the hot water faucet, the pipeline will feel hot to the touch and should have a red handle on it. This enables you to turn off the water. The cold water line will feel cold to the touch and will have a black or blue handle. Once the water has been turned off, open the faucet and let the remaining water run out.

If the faucet is cross- or X-shaped, with four elements extending from the center, there should be a small ceramic decorative button in the center. Remove this button and you will find a screw head. This is what holds the handle on. Remove the screw and then the handle.

Next, there should be a large, six-sided chrome nut that fits up against the sink itself. Unscrew this and remove it. In some cases, with older units, this could be a porcelain cover that doesn't require unscrewing. Simply remove it. A nut, called a packing nut, should be underneath. Next is a round piece of fiber, plastic or rubber and a larger packing washer. There could be two elements to the packing washer. Remove these and set them aside. As you do, inspect them. These are several of the elements that may need replacing.

At this point, you will encounter the stem of the faucet. It is a round metal rod over which were slipped the various elements that have been removed. However, at the other end, the stem widens to reveal a threaded portion. At the tip, a metal piece into which should be fitted a rubber washer is secured by a screw. Replace the washer. If the screw sticks, use a penetrating oil and let it sit for half an hour before trying to turn the screw again.

The washers and the packing are what permit leaks. You will want to replace both washers and packing at the same time. They cost only a few cents, and the parts are fairly standard at any hardware store. If you have been able to describe the faucet to the hardware store person, he or she probably will have provided a supply of several washers and packing units. You should be able to select from the assortment. If not, take the washers and packing to the hardware store, *remembering the order they came in*, and replace them. Then replace each element just as it was removed and turn the water back on. If these directions were followed the leak should have stopped.

A slightly newer version of the stem faucet has two handles and a common spout. The water comes together from two separate faucets *after* it reaches the spout. In the more modern single-lever faucet, hot and cold water come together *before* entering the faucet unit.

For the stem faucet with two handles, a single spout and a drain pull in one unit, begin by turning off the water under the sink; red handle for hot, blue or black for cold. Then pry up the decorative top from each handle to reveal a small screw. Remove the screw and then the handle itself.

Now, instead of the packing nut in the previous version, you are likely to encounter a locknut. Use a wrench to turn the locknut counterclockwise. At this point, one of two things should happen. Either the stem will come out with the locknut or the stem will remain in the faucet. In the case of the latter, replace the handle, then turn it slowly until the stem unscrews and can be removed.

You will be able to determine whether the washer is flat, beveled, includes a spring or is a diaphragm type. Replace it in kind. If the leaking doesn't stop after the washer or washers have been replaced, there may be a problem with the faucet seating unit. This is what presses up against the washer. If it is marred, scratched or otherwise rough to the touch, it should be replaced. As this requires a special tool and special effort, I suggest that you report your findings to the management or maintenance people and put up with the dripping for a while.

Next is the newer, single-lever faucet. Here you will have to find what is called a "setscrew" to remove the handle and get at the problem. On the ball-type lever, the setscrew should be under the handle. Removing it requires an Allen wrench. This is a small, inexpensive, six-sided, L-shaped piece of metal. It comes in several sizes. You will have to test several sizes to determine which fits, in that sizes are not indicated. Insert the short part of the L in a hole in the underpart of the faucet that has a screw set in it (hence the term "setscrew"). This doesn't look like the kind of standard screw with which you are familiar. The setscrew holds the handle to the rest of the faucet. *Do not remove the setscrew entirely.* It is small and could easily get lost. (Caution: setscrews come in various sizes. You will be wise to purchase an assortment of Allen wrenches, because the next setscrew you come in contact with undoubtedly will be of a different size. They are inexpensive, costing about $3.95, and come five or six in a small pouch.)

Once the handle is removed, a metal cap must be unscrewed. Beneath this is a plastic cam assembly. This fits into the brass faucet and has a little nib that fits in a slot. Remove this carefully. Under it is a beveled washer. Remove that.

Next is a round metal or plastic ball with a lever sticking out of it. This lever is the one that extended through the plastic cam and the washer you have just removed. Remove the ball and inspect it. If it is rough and corroded, it needs replacing. It may simply require cleaning.

After all the elements have been cleaned or replaced, if the water still drips, repeat the process and replace the valve seats and springs. These were underneath the ball when you removed it. This, too, is a simple process. Use a long-nose pliers and carefully remove the springs and valve seats. Replace them in kind. Then fit the ball back into the opening, being careful to note that there is a nib protruding from the side of the ball cavity. The nib fits into an opening on the side of the ball. *This is vital.* Finally, replace the elements as they were removed. Tighten the cap assembly and reconnect the faucet handle. You should be drip-free.

Shower Heads: Sometimes shower heads clog from high

mineral content in the water. If so, after disassembling the unit, soak the parts in vinegar. Using a toothpick or a needle, poke the tiny spray holes to get rid of the mineral deposits. If you have a dripping from the shower head, replace the "O" ring, which fits between the swivel ball and the shower head. This is another form of washer. Disconnecting the shower head is a very simple process.

Running Toilet: First, try bending the metal rod that connects the float ball (the large round metal or plastic "ball" that floats on top of the water and rises and falls with the water level). Make this adjustment when water flows over the top of the overflow pipe. Bend the rod slightly downward. The water should stop rising just below the top of the overflow pipe the next time you flush the toilet. If not, there may be water inside the float. Remove the float by unscrewing it from the rod. Shake it to determine if there is water inside. If there is, replace it. New floats can be obtained at any hardware store.

If water seems to be leaking from the tank into the bowl, accompanied by a gurgling sound, there may be a problem with the outlet valve. Turn off the water to the tank by using the handle below the tank and behind the bowl. Then flush the toilet to remove the water from the tank. Now, lift up the rubber or plastic disc that is sitting at the bottom of the tank next to the overflow pipe with a thin piece of metal rising from its top. Clean the disc and the outlet beneath it of any grime and mineral deposits. The problem could be that the disc or ball simply isn't seating correctly in the valve.

Check the disc. It should be firm, not mushy to the feel. If you suspect the disc is not seating well because it is not firm enough, replace it. If the unit is old and the leaking doesn't stop, even with replacement of the disc, consider replacing the unit with what is called a flapped ball. This has a hinge and is attached to the overflow pipe. It should always provide a good fit.

Toilet Seats: This usually is another simple job. Unless the bolts that hold the toilet seat on are rusted and corroded, they should be easily replaceable. New seats don't use metal bolts or nuts anymore. They use plastic. The toilet seat is connected with two bolts and two nuts. In some cases, the nut is recessed into the porcelain fixture. This could require the use of a socket wrench to make it secure, but in the years that I have replaced toilet seats, I have never come across one I couldn't tighten to my satisfaction using only my fingers. Give it a try. It it isn't tight enough, ask the maintenance person to drop by at his convenience and give it an extra twist.

Clogged Drains: This can be caused by many things. Primary is a buildup of grease, hair, soap scum and food particles, which shouldn't have gone down the drain in the first place. For this kind of problem, try a liquid drain cleanser like Drāno or Liquid Plummer. READ THE DIRECTIONS CAREFULLY.

Some forms of liquid cleaner shouldn't be used with some surfaces. Make certain you know from the directions and warnings on the container what the cleaner can and can't be used for. One or two applications will take care of most routine drain clogging.

If the toilet bowl or bathtub is clogged, first try a rubber plunger, often referred to as "the plumber's helper," by applying a steady push–pull action. Pump the plunger up and down about ten times, then pull the plunger up quickly. Repeat this procedure several times if necessary. Make certain that there is no air getting into the drain opening as you are pumping. To protect against this, fill the tub or sink with enough water to cover the plunger. Be careful, however—the water can splash.

Never use a drain cleaner with a plunger. If the plunger hasn't worked, try a liquid drain cleaner. Some products of this sort will damage the unit or the pipe, so be certain you have read the directions.

Another option, if you are working at a sink, is to remove the drain trap. This is the U-shaped stainless unit directly under the drain. It should have two six-sided slip nuts, which have to be unscrewed. Place a pail under the U-shaped pipe to catch the water that will drain out once the two nuts are unscrewed. On some units, there will be a "clean-out plug" at the bottom of the U-shaped unit. This plug can be removed, and then, with a coat hanger, you can fish out debris that may be stuck in the outflow section of the pipe, preventing the water from flowing smoothly. DO NOT, UNDER ANY CIRCUMSTANCES, REMOVE A

TRAP OR A TRAP PLUG IF YOU HAVE USED A LIQUID OR CRYSTAL DRAIN CLEANER RECENTLY. THIS COULD BE EXTREMELY DANGEROUS.

Among the many books dealing with home repairs, I found the following most helpful:

- *Reader's Digest House Improvement Manual*, Reader's Digest.
- *New York Times Complete Manual of Home Repairs*, by Bernard Gladstone, Macmillan.
- *Super Handyman's Encyclopedia of Home Repair Hints*, by A. Carrell, Prentice-Hall, Inc.
- *Home Repairs and Improvement Series*, Time-Life Books.

4

Casting Your Bread: Money Management

Most of us, no matter how much we earn, aren't going to have as much money as we think is needed to accommodate the way we want to live. For people just starting out, that is likely to be especially true.

This chapter briefly presents some things to think about on money management subjects: setting up a budget, fixed and variable expenses, record keeping, impulse buying, ways to help make money go farther, interest and taxes, setting priorities and how to get help in managing money if you need it.

Working with What You Have

The key to any money management program is determing exactly how much money you have to work with. Remember, a starting salary of $12,000, $15,000 or $18,000 is *gross* pay. A number of items will be deducted from this amount and the *net* pay will be substantively less.

The largest deductions will be for federal, state and possibly

local income taxes and for Social Security tax. If you have no
dependents and you earn $12,000 a year in New Jersey, you will
pay $56.20 in federal income tax and $20.60 in state tax each
two-week pay period. Whether local tax is deducted depends
upon local tax codes. Social Security taxes will reduce gross
salary by another $30.92. Take-home pay would then be
$353.81. The following chart supplied by a tax accountant lists
the federal, state and Social Security tax bite in seven representative states and the District of Columbia for people earning
$12,000, $15,000 and $18,000 annually in 1983.

Your Annual Tax Bite

	$12,000	$15,000	$18,000
Salary, single individual	$12,000	$15,000	$18,000
Federal taxes (Biweekly)	56.20	75.20	103.80
Social Security taxes (Biweekly)	30.92	38.65	46.39
State taxes			
California	11.42	18.20	26.60
District of Columbia	24.99	34.70	45.18
Illinois	10.58	13.46	16.34
Massachusetts	20.26	26.46	32.66
Michigan	25.64	32.97	40.30
New York	20.60	30.29	41.59
Pennsylvania	11.31	14.14	16.96
Texas	-0-	-0-	-0-

Here is a tip regarding federal and state withholding taxes.
You are asked to fill out a form at the time you are employed that
states how many dependents you have. Normally, if you are
single, you would state one. However, for tax purposes, you
have the option of claiming up to fourteen dependents, despite
the fact that you have none. The more dependents, the less the
withholding. (If you claim fourteen dependents, your employer
is required to notify the IRS. Further, if you earn more than
$200 a week and do not want federal income tax withheld, the
IRS will be notified.)

Why claim dependents you don't have? If you deduct too little, you will not have paid enough taxes when it comes time to file your income tax forms. Some people resent the government using their money during the year when taxes aren't due until April 15. They prefer to have the money, use it as they wish, and pay taxes when they are due. (Note: the IRS requires that 80 percent of federal income tax be paid by the end of each year.)

The thinking is that they will invest several hundred dollars each month in some form of savings and earn interest. But many people won't or can't put the theory to work and don't have the discipline to save and invest each month. What kind of person you are will determine what you should do about this approach to taxation. You may wish to explore this option with a tax attorney or accountant.

In addition to these deductions, you could have others for health insurance, group life insurance, a pension plan contribution, union or professional dues and for a local federated charity, such as United Way.

Your take-home pay is what you have left after these deductions. For many people, it is a shock. But shock or not, this is what you have to live on until your next paycheck. How well one lives depends upon planning and what there is to work with.

Earlier, I stated that most people leaving home for the first time seem to have only the vaguest notion of how to get along financially once they are out on their own. This belief has been corroborated by statements from countless young people during the course of my interviews.

Karen C.: "Although I didn't like it at the time, I really appreciate the fact that my parents made me sit down and work through *in detail* how much money I would need to get started on my own. I was just thinking how great it would be to have an apartment, to be able to entertain and to be away from restrictions at home. They made me figure out how much I would have to have *in hand* when I walked out the door. Then I had to figure out what it would cost me each month for all the things that living requires. Once I compared this with what I was earning, I could see that a beginning job in a bank simply wasn't going to provide enough money. I would have to have a second job, at least for a while. It wasn't much fun, and I got angry and frustrated, but I sure would have been in trouble if they hadn't taken the time to work it through with me. I just wanted to get out on my own."

Establishing a Budget

Begin by setting up a budget. You control your money. This is a comforting feeling. A well–set up budget will help you avoid getting into debt, provide for niceties from time to time and, for the most part, help avoid cash flow crunches.

There are three kinds of expenditures: fixed, variable and discretionary. Fixed are those that are the same each month. Variable are those where the amount can be controlled more easily but that must be considered as regular or periodic expenditures. Discretionary expenses are the things you choose to spend money on but that are neither regular nor required. This category includes luxuries.

THE BUDGET FORMAT

First, make a list of all items that make up your income each month. Then list regular monthly expenses for rent, heating, gas, electricity, water, trash collection, *basic* phone charges, insurance, auto payments, student loan payments, personal loan payments and anything else you must pay on a *regular monthly basis* and is a *fixed or standard amount*.

Next, list those things for which you expend money each month *for which the amount varies or may vary*. This includes: food, clothing, gas, oil and repairs for your car, medical and dental bills, long distance phone charges, commuter transportation charges if you take the train or a bus, lunches and gifts for birthdays or other occasions. The chart below provides a format for helping to determine how your income is being used each month.

Income and Expense Statement

INCOME: Money you receive.

GROSS SALARY/WAGES	$_____
LESS REGULAR DEDUCTIONS: Withholding tax, Social Security (FICA), health insurance, etc.	− $_____
TAKE-HOME PAY	$_____
COMMISSIONS, TIPS, BONUSES	$_____
INTEREST OR DIVIDENDS: Savings, stocks, bonds, other securities, notes.	$_____
REFUNDS/REBATES	$_____
CASH GIFTS	$_____
OTHER INCOME	$_____
INCOME FROM TRUSTS	$_____
ROYALTIES/RESIDUALS	$_____
TOTAL AVAILABLE INCOME	$_____

FIXED EXPENSES: Payments you must make, usually set by written agreement, at regular times for set amounts. Also included are self-established savings goals.

RENT OR MORTGAGE PAYMENTS: Include property tax, if any, and insurance if automatically included in payment.	$_____
UTILITIES: Gas, electricity, heating, water, garbage.	$_____
SAVINGS: Regular savings accounts, Christmas club, time deposit accounts, savings bonds, etc.	$_____
INSTALLMENT CONTRACT PAYMENTS: Fixed payments made at regular intervals over specific time periods for purchase of vehicles, furniture, student loans, etc.	$_____

TELEPHONE: Basic monthly phone
charges. $_____

INSURANCE: Personal property, tenant's,
auto, liability, life, health, other. $_____

REGULAR CONTRIBUTIONS: Church,
charities, etc. $_____

DUES: Union, club, other memberships. $_____

TOTAL FIXED EXPENSES $_____

VARIABLE EXPENSES: Regular expenses that may fluctuate
from month to month or year to year.

CHARGE ACCOUNTS: Store account and
credit card payments. $_____

MEDICAL/DENTAL: Drugs and
treatment not covered by insurance. $_____

TRANSPORTATION: Car operating
expenses (gas, oil, repairs, servicing),
parking, public transportation. $_____

HOUSEHOLD
MAINTENANCE/REPAIR: Cleaning,
apartment/appliance repairs (material,
labor). $_____

FOOD: Groceries, nonfood items in
supermarket bill. $_____

PERSONAL MAINTENANCE: Clothing,
laundry, barber, beauty salon, health and
beauty products. $_____

TOTAL VARIABLE EXPENSES $_____

TOTAL AVAILABLE INCOME $_____

LESS FIXED AND VARIABLE TOTAL
EXPENSES   − $_____

AMOUNT available for additional
savings, investments, debt payment or
luxuries (discretionary) $_____

DISCRETIONARY EXPENSES: Amounts expended,
               if available, for non-necessities.

SELF-IMPROVEMENT/EDUCATION:
Books, magazines, newspapers, seminars,
lessons, tuition. $_____
RECREATION/ENTERTAINMENT:
Restaurants, movies, sports, vacations,
weekends, parties, etc. $_____
OTHERS: $_____
     TOTAL DISCRETIONARY
     EXPENSES $_____
     TOTAL EXPENSES
     (FIXED, VARIABLE AND
     DISCRETIONARY) $_____

Do not exclude an amount for savings purposes. Further, no matter how small, I urge you to keep this amount up front in your fixed expense list so it gets the attention it deserves. Lack of savings is one of the biggest problems most people face. Many individuals wonder why, after years of working, they have no money to invest. One answer is that they have failed to set up a savings system. Don't let this happen to you. Money should be saved each pay period and periodically invested in some form of safe, high-interest savings instrument (See Chapter 6).

Once fixed and variable expenses are totaled, you will know how much is left for discretionary use. This includes such items as entertainment, extra clothing, recreational activity, flowers for a friend, self-improvement courses, books, magazines, parties, liquor, etc.

The key to developing discretionary funds is to control the

variable expenditures. For instance, cut back on trips to the hair stylist, write notes instead of making long distance calls to reduce expenses and provide some of the extras you'd like. It is a matter of trade-offs. There is only so much money to work with.

Planning Ahead

Another aspect of money management is looking ahead to the forthcoming year to anticipate expenditures. If tires on the car need replacing for the winter months, start planning for that expense well in advance. Semiannual dental checkups can be handled the same way. Schedule vacations ahead of time and budget a small amount each month so the expense isn't overwhelming when the time comes. If plans include returning to night school in the fall, be sure to factor that in as part of fall and winter monthly payments, if that is the way you plan to handle the matter.

Once a budget has been set, stick to it faithfully. This way you'll avoid having to bankrupt yourself in any given month with huge payments for something that could have been foreseen. If a $500 life insurance premium is due in December and there are holiday presents to buy as well, you won't have to worry. By setting aside insurance payments each month for ten months, the cost has been spread wisely, and December holiday expenditures are now within reason.

Establishing Priorities

Another important aspect is setting priorities. You won't be able to afford everything and will have to weigh "needs" against "wants." You'll also have to prioritize needs; a chair versus a winter coat, for instance.

Periodically, look back at your budget to see where the money went. A surprisingly large amount is likely to be unaccounted for. This represents money that was taken in cash, stuck in your pocket or pocketbook and spent as the needs arose. Much is spent for impulse items, such as soda, snacks, gum, etc., some for drugs or cosmetics at the drug store, some for cigarettes or entertainment.

Each day for the next two weeks, keep track of every expenditure. Don't ignore or exclude anything. Then, at the end of the two weeks, review the list. Chances are you'll be shocked. But this will give you a pretty good indication of how the little things add up.

For instance, if you are a smoker and you put away a pack a day, that's $365 a year. If you are an ice cream freak, three cones a week at about 85¢ a cone amounts to over $130 a year. Drinks, at anywhere from $1.50 to $3.50 each, can put a heavy dent in your budget in just a few evenings. The expenses add up quickly and are part of discretionary income. By choosing ice cream or booze, you are giving up something else. As always, in establishing priorities, the choice is yours.

IMPULSE BUYING

Financial counselors stress that one of the most certain ways to throw a budget off balance and put yourself in debt is to succumb to impulse buying. Retailers know customers are subject to impulse purchasing, and so they arrange their wares to capitalize on it.

One way to help curb this tendency is resisting the purchase the moment it looks most attractive. Then resolve to return the next day and buy the item. If you are willing to do this, the purchase is probably worthwhile. Most people will overcome the impulse and not go back to the store.

Another way to resist impulse buying, which I use on occasion, is to make a purchase and take the item home. Put it away and don't unwrap it. Examine the purchase in a day or so and see if you are still enthusiastic about it. You may be surprised.

Obviously, the best way to avoid impulse buying is to stay out of certain stores unless you know specifically what you need. Then go where you can find that item and make the purchase. If you want to comparison- or window-shop to kill some time or for the fun of it, leave your money and charge cards at home.

Credit Cards

Credit cards can be a mixed blessing. On the one hand, they help you to manage money by: permitting you to avoid carrying cash, bypassing the need to produce reams of identification (as when paying for something by check), providing receipts for purchase, creating a record for refund or tax purposes, helping with bookkeeping and establishing credit. Some cards provide a cash resource that can be used like a loan. Credit cards admittedly are convenient.

On the other hand, with credit cards, charging items sometimes becomes too easy. Somehow, it doesn't seem quite the same as writing a check or paying cash. Further, unless purchases are paid within a certain time after receiving the bill, they incur finance charges. And in most states, one has to pay an annual fee to obtain a credit card, whether it is used or not.

There are several kinds of credit cards. Some, like Visa and MasterCard, are issued by financial institutions. Others, like those supplied by department stores, specialty stores, auto rental companies, oil companies and the phone company, are designed for use at their facilities for their products and are not usable at a variety of places.

Visa and MasterCard are referred to as general-purpose cards, while those issued by Gulf or Exxon, Bloomingdale's or I. Magnin, Sears or J. C. Penny, Hertz or Avis are dedicated, or single-purpose, cards.

The third kind is the travel and entertainment card. These are issued by American Express, Diners Club and Carte Blanche. They require charges to be paid promptly and in full each month.

Some people seem to pride themselves on how many credit cards they can accumulate. One fellow, in his early thirties, with a wife and two small children, earns in excess of $25,000 a year.

They have thirty-two credit cards, including two MasterCards and three Visas, each with at least a $1,000 credit line. The most liberal financial advisor will spot this as potential trouble. This man's obligations and paycheck are currently in tune, but exercizing his credit options without restraint will quickly promote financial difficulty.

Charles P., Consumer credit counselor: "Credit should be considered a privilege. It should be used sparingly, for emergencies or when you are caught short on cash, but not as a substitute for money you don't have."

A couple words of advice: To protect yourself from overspending, make sure there is enough money in the bank to cover the charge when it is made. Charged items are easy to forget; when the bills arrive, don't be stuck wondering how to pay them.

Ginny R.:   "Be careful of credit cards. They can be bad if you let them get away from you. I saved quite a bit of money before coming here but went through it all in three months, mainly by charging things I shouldn't have. I learned the hard way."

Be aware that credit cards or travel and entertainment cards belong to the issuer, not to you. And if the credit they provide is abused, they have the right to request that the card be surrendered to them.

Mary W.:   "I had a credit card and satisfactory credit. We had moved to this community from another state, and I wanted to buy some plants to decorate the apartment. At the store, they took my credit card, called someone on the phone to verify it, and then told me they couldn't accept the card. I was so embarrassed! No explanation, just that they couldn't accept the charge. What was even more embarrassing and frustrating was that they *kept* the card. The girl at the counter told me the people on the phone said to keep the card. I told her it was my card and I wanted it back. She told me the card belonged to the bank that issued it. I was furious, but she was right. I subsequently talked to the bank and straightened things out, but it was an experience I never want to go through again."

One of the disadvantages of having a credit card is that in virtually every instance you pay a substantial fee for the privilege of having and using one. Depending upon the card, the state in which it was issued and the laws of that state relative to interest rates, you can pay from zero to $45 annually. Also, annual finance charges on the balances maintained in the account can amount to 12 to 18 percent.

With most charge cards, as long as the balance is paid upon receipt of the bill, no finance charges are incurred. All cards require a specified minimum payment or payment in full each month. The card can be revoked for noncompliance at any time.

Often it takes from several weeks to a month before charges are processed and invoiced. A dinner charged in mid July may not show up on your invoice until September, for instance. Then you have a certain number of days in which to pay the invoice. By charging, you were able to keep the money almost three months before paying for the dinner you had in July. If you are a shrewd money manager, you can use this knowledge to your advantage.

A typical Visa or MasterCard contract lists two interest rates. First is for the advance of cash or for loan checks. (Loan checks enable you to write a loan on a special check, issued by the bank, that is charged to your credit card.) This generally is less than on the second rate for *purchases* charged. Interest rate ceilings are regulated by the state in which you reside or in which you have obtained credit.

Either way and no matter how you look at it, the annual interest charge on credit cards can be a lot of money. If a $700 charge balance is maintained each month for a year, you would pay $105 in interest, computed at 15 percent. If, on the other hand, you invested the $700 at 6 percent, you would earn $42.

If you can't avoid making a purchase, consider borrowing the money from your bankcard and paying cash for the purchase. You'll save several percentage points in interest.

CREDIT CARD LIABILITY

As a good money manager, if you are going to use credit cards, know the extent of financial liability in the event the card or cards are lost or stolen.

Truth-in-lending laws offer some protection. When a card is

issued, it will contain information regarding lost or stolen cards. Read it carefully. In short, what it says is the following.

* If a card is lost or stolen, notify the card issuer immediately by phone or by letter. Notification by letter is better: You have a record.
* If you've notified the issuer, your legal liability is $50 per card for any unauthorized use.
* If you have a duplicate card, it must be surrendered to the issuer.
* You will be issued a new card shortly (assuming your credit is good).

To protect yourself, make a list of all credit cards, with the number, the expiration date and the name and address of the issuer. Most card issuers have a phone number either on the card or as part of the material accompanying the card. Keep this information in a safe, separate location for possible future reference.

Remember: *If the card company isn't notified when the card is lost, the liability for expenditures made with the card is yours.*

It is possible to purchase lost or stolen credit card protection from an insurer. You pay a modest annual fee and provide the company with the name and number of each card. If the cards are lost, simply notify the company. They go through all the trouble of notifying each card issuer. If you have ten or fifteen cards, the amount of effort to notify each could be significant. This is particularly true if you are on a trip and your list is at home. It is a good service.

Special Expenditures

AIR TRAVEL

When traveling, always check on the variety of fares. Don't accept the first rate quoted. Airline fare rates change often; be aware that there may be a large number of options that provide significant savings. Here are some important facts to keep in mind:

- *If you are vacationing, avoid flying during the height of the tourist season.* Costs of air travel to Florida or Southern California in winter will be higher than during off-season, for example. Ask when rates change in the spring or fall and schedule travel just before or afterward.
- *Buy your ticket in advance.* Fares often are reduced if purchased seven to thirty days early.
- *Fly standby.* This means arriving at the airport without a ticket and seeing if there is room on a flight to your destination.
- *Check out Super-Saver fares.* Usually, these require purchasing the ticket in advance and staying at your destination at least seven days. These are among the most economical flight arrangements.
- *Fly off-peak days.* If you depart and return during the middle of the week, you can save. But check with your travel agent on this; various airlines define "the middle of the week" differently.
- *Inquire about special promotional fares.* These are based on availability.
- *Take advantage of packages or charter trips.* While you can save, charters can be canceled or the times changed; you will have no recourse. Some governments underwrite the costs of travel packages, to Jamaica or Mexico, for instance. Investigate the contents of these packages so you are aware of your obligations. Sometimes you can hook up with a tour that has extra seats. You need not stay with the group once it is on the ground. If you are traveling alone, this may be a good way to meet people.

Travel Agents

Not for monetary management reasons alone, I suggest you use a travel agency for travel plans. First, the agency makes its money from the airlines, cruise ships, hotels and auto rental agencies with which they do business, not from you. Agency people are professionally trained to know all the ins and outs of a complicated business. They can save you money, time and aggravation and will provide suggestions regarding things you might not have thought of or couldn't have known. Finally, they will be able to assist you in obtaining passports and visas and will be aware of what inoculations you may need in a foreign country. Using a travel agent can be a good investment.

TRAINS AND BUSES

If you are commuting between two cities where you have the option of bus or rail service, think about buses. Today buses are large, clean, have restroom facilities, are less expensive than trains and have regular service between major communities. If you haven't taken a bus recently, you may be surprised.

If you are traveling between Washington, DC, and New York City, going by Greyhound Bus will cost $24.50 one way. By regular Amtrak train, the cost is $37 and by high speed Metroliner, $46. The saving is obvious. From Chicago to Philadelphia by Greyhound is $70, and by Amtrak train, it is $105.

AUTOMOBILES

To buy, to rent, to lease—that is the question. For most people, a set of wheels seems like a passport to freedom, an absolute necessity. It also is a major expense. Before rushing out to purchase a car, especially a new one, take a look at the economics.

Purchasing. First, if you buy a new car, consider the reason for the purchase. Do you really need to shell out $6,000 to $10,000 for automobile transportation? Or is it the symbolism, attractiveness and desire to own something new that provides the motivation? How much traveling are you going to be doing? Will the car be used primarily to commute to work? Is that expensive commuting? Will you need a garage, or will it be parked outside in all kinds of weather? Will insurance be higher because it is new, a sports car or because you are using it for commutation? In short, are you running up unnecessary costs for ego reasons? Could the money be used to better advantage?

Buying a new car may not be the best management of your money. Let's explore that a bit further.

Unless you possess unusual financial resources, you will be financing most of the cost of a new car. The finance charge can be substantial, even though you are permitted to deduct the interest from your federal income taxes if you file the long form. You will have to maintain the car. This includes regular check-ups, new tires when needed and other repairs required from time to time. It also will have to be insured.

Now, consider the following example. Say you purchase a car for $8,000, with a $2,000 down payment. You must finance the additional $6,000. At current lending rates for a four-year period, the cost of financing a new car would be $163.20 per month, including principal and interest, a total of $7,833.60.

Next, we checked with the American Automobile Association to determine current estimated average costs for gas, oil and routine maintenance per month across the nation. Added to this was insurance, depreciation, licensing and taxes. The figure provided was $155.34, based on a six-cylinder, midsize car driven by an adult primarily for pleasure up to 15,000 miles per year.

So, you can expect to pay about $318.54 a month for the use of a new automobile. The questions are: can you afford it, and for your needs, is this the smart way to manage your transportation money?

Another option is a used car. Spending several thousand dollars less initially and reducing the monthly payments often puts someone in the driver's seat. The drawbacks here are that you may be buying someone else's problems and thus repairs, and you may be getting a car that has a lower fuel-efficiency rating, thereby costing more for gasoline.

Leasing.   What alternatives do you have? First, leasing a car lessens the initial outlay. While leasing may cost more per month, the new car of your choice can be obtained without the large up-front payment. The amount otherwise set aside for the down payment can then be invested and earning interest. If you are not filing the long income tax form, you won't be able to take advantage of interest deductions, so leasing may not have an added advantage in that respect.

A major auto leasing company in a large eastern city recently advertised the following monthly rates, with no down payment, a $300 security deposit, for forty-eight months on a closed-end lease:

Toyota Tercel, Honda CRX, Mazda GLC, Nissan Sentra or Pulsar, Subaru, Olds Omega and Chevy Cavalier ... $159

Toyota Camry, Ford Thunderbird, Datsun 200SX, Honda Accord and Chevy Citation $199

Pontiac Trans Am, Olds Ninety-eight Regency, Honda Prelude, Toyota Cressida, Buick LeSabre and Chevy Caprice $259

Rental. The next option is to rent a car when it is needed. Car or van pooling to work and taking the bus or train will result in additional savings. If a car is needed on weekends, rent one.

Rentals vary depending upon the company, length of time you want the vehicle, its size and how it is to be used. A compact car can be rented for two full days for as little as $49 plus 15¢ a mile on the weekend. Renting each Saturday and Sunday for four weeks will cost $196 (plus mileage). Compare this against the cost of a three-year lease ($238 a month, plus gas and oil) or the fee for buying and financing a new model ($163, plus gas and oil, per month). On the lease and purchase arrangement, there still are charges for repairs, registration, insurance, taxes and an initial down payment. The choice, as always, is yours.

There are a number of excellent publications that evaluate the operational costs of automobiles and can assist you in making the decision once you come down to it. Here are several that may be helpful if you are interested in delving further into the intricacies of owning and operating an automobile.

Among the many books on purchasing automobiles you may find the following helpful:

• *Edmund's New Car Prices*, Edmund's Publishing Corp.
• *Edmund's Used Car Prices*, Edmund's Publishing Corp.

- *Consumer Guide to New Cars*, Signet.
- *Consumer Reports Guide to Used Cars*, Consumer Reports.
- *Consumer Reports Guide to New Cars*, Consumer Reports.
- *How to Beat the Car Dealer at His Own Game*, by L. J. Brum, B.M. Consumer Publications.
- *Consumer Guide to Car Buying*, National Highway Safety Administration.
- *N.A.D.A. Official Used Car Guide*, National Automobile Dealers' Association (published monthly; includes average retail prices, average trade in price, average loan and insurance rating).

Taxes

In managing money, people encounter a variety of hidden taxes. Perhaps the one that demands most of our income is the sales tax. Some states don't have sales taxes, most do. They range from 3 to 6 percent, and vary widely in how they are applied. However, this is deductible from your federal income taxes. The Internal Revenue Service even provides a table in the back of the tax preparation guide sent with your tax forms. However, if you have purchased an automobile, several large pieces of furniture or other expensive items, keep track of *all* sales receipts. Then determine whether the sales taxes you paid exceed that allowed in the tables. If they do and you possess documentation, add the tax from the extraordinary items to the amount in the table and use it as a deduction.

If you earn over $25,000, have made any major purchases, own property or have paid any unusual interest on a loan or mortgage, seriously consider hiring an accountant. As professionals, they will know the latest tax information and could save a considerable amount of money in preparing your returns. Their fees are deductible.

Thirty-Six Money-Saving Tips

While there are countless ways to save money, from replacing heels and soles of shoes to putting slip covers on worn furniture, here are some that I recommend:

1. When buying large appliances, ask about floor samples, discounted models or slightly damaged or scratched models. Sometimes you can obtain items that have been repaired and never picked up. The repair shop often will sell it for the price of the repairs.

2. When buying bakery goods, bakery thrift shops sell day-old items at as much as 40 percent off; usually the same quality as products in the stores.

3. Use self-service gas pumps. Once a month, visit the full-service pump to get oil and tire pressure checked, but keep your purchase at a minimum. Come back the next day to fill up.

4. Remove unnecessary items from the trunk and backseat of car. Extra weight means less gas mileage per gallon.

5. Keep tires inflated at the recommended pressure. This can save 2 to 3 miles per gallon of gas.

6. Avoid the emergency room at the hospital for anything but true emergencies. Emergency room costs are expensive and treatment may not be covered by your insurance unless it is done by your doctor in his/her office.

7. Shop for both prescription and nonprescription drugs. There can be significant differences between local neighborhood drug stores and the large chains.

8. When your doctor prescribes drugs, ask about generic versus brand-name drugs. Generics contain the same ingredients but often cost half as much.

9. If an item you want is not on sale, inquire when the next sale will be held. Sales take place almost monthly, and by waiting a few days or a week, you may be able to save 20 to 40 percent.

10. When using the long income tax form, deduct the value of old clothing, books, etc. donated to charity. Get a receipt for what you think it is worth.

11. When buying carpeting, look for large remnants. Often you can save substantially. Look for carpet discounters as well.

12. Learn to do simple home repairs, unless your landlord will have them done for you without charge. Service calls are costly.

13. Process film by mail. This can save you as much as 50 percent over film processed by regular camera shops, drug or food stores. In any case, compare cost.

14. Make long distance calls during off-peak hours. After 11:00 in the evening and before 8:00 in the morning are cheapest. Weekends are cheaper than weekdays. Better still, if you make a lot of long distance calls, investigate a long distance discount service, such as MCI or Sprint, and save even more (See Chapter 5).

15. Avoid calling collect, person to person or using a telephone credit card. All are more expensive than station-to-station calls.

16. Phone companies have several levels of service, at different monthly rates. Determine the number of calls you expect to make and the area within which they will be made. Avoid buying more service than you need.

17. Drink water with your dinner meal. By eliminating wine or soda, you'll save money *and* lose weight.

18. Brown bag your lunch unless you have a date or business luncheon. It is a lot cheaper than eating out. And who knows who you could meet on a park bench?

19. Take home doggie bags from restaurants. They often provide a second, equally delicious meal a day or so later.

20. Use shopping coupons for all your needs, from "twofers" at McDonalds to pantyhose specials to food at the supermarket. And watch for double coupon values at the food stores.

21. Collect recipes that use rice and pasta and cut out meat. Add beans and you can get the same amount of protein without the meat at far less cost. Try Oriental and Middle Eastern recipes.

22. If you are sending gifts to young children, wrap them in the color comics section of the Sunday paper. Kids enjoy this, and the paper doesn't cost extra.

23. If you work for a fairly sizable company, ask the purchasing department if they sell old desks, typewriters or furniture. You may be able to turn up a bargain.

24. If you can afford it, buy larger sizes of liquor and mixes. Don't always buy the best-known names; most people don't know the difference.

25. If your bank has an automatic teller machine (ATM), use it to get cash rather than writing checks for cash. ATM transactions still don't cost anything at most banks.

26. If you are taking out a loan, avoid credit life and credit accident insurance. This can be an extremely expensive purchase for what you are getting. You are better off buying a small standard term insurance policy for the amount financed instead and reduce the amount each year.

27. If you need to borrow money and you have whole life insurance, check how much is available for a loan. The rates will be better than anyplace else. Finance company rates are highest.

28. Increase the deductible on your auto insurance. You will have to pay a larger portion if you have a claim, but the annual premium will be reduced.

29. If you are paying for heat, turn the thermostat down to 65 degrees when you leave in the morning and up to 70 when you return. Turn it down again when you go to bed and up when you arise.

30. Don't buy books unless you want them in your permanent library. Otherwise, be terribly selective and use the public library. Before paying full price, try a discount bookstore.

31. Don't be afraid to buy imperfects and seconds of certain items, like socks, towels, underwear, etc.

32. Shop at discount stores or so-called "dime stores" for routine items, like kitchen ware, sweatshirts and pants, and items you intend to use once or twice where quality is not mandatory.

33. Read publications such as *Consumer Reports* at your library before making purchases of appliances and other "big ticket" items.

34. Avoid buying eyeglasses from an optician connected with your eye doctor. Shop for a discount eyewear store where frames are less costly and the expense is in grinding the lenses.

35. Think twice before investing a lot of money in apartment furnishings. A future roommate or spouse may own similar items. Some of your belongings may be discarded to make room for theirs. You never know what will survive when the move together is accomplished. Travel light until you know your living arrangements.

36. For the most part, conventional retail stores charge top dollar. Never pay these prices until you have exhausted all other avenues, such as sales, discounters, factory outlets, distressed

merchandise, secondhand stores, garage and yard sales, auctions, ads in the paper, etc.

There are many good books on managing your money. Some of the better ones are contained in the following list:

- *Sylvia Porter's Money Book*, by Sylvia Porter, *Avon*.
- *Everybody's Money Book*, by Jane Bryant Quinn, *Delacorte Press*.
- *Women and Money*, by Mary Rogers and Nancy Joyce, McGraw-Hill.
- *New York Times Book of Money*, Robert Blodgett, New York Times Book Co.

5

Consumer Smarts: Buying Wisely

Now that a place to live has been found, some efforts made to paint and furnish it and some thought given to managing your money, you'll be confronted with a number of other buying decisions. For that matter, as a consumer, you'll be making similar choices for the rest of your life. Now is a good time to develop some consumer awareness that will help in making informed decisions and in getting your money's worth. This way you won't get taken, and in the event that a consumer problem arises, you'll know what to do about it.

DON'T BUY IT IF YOU DON'T NEED IT

The business of business is to make items or provide services people will buy and use. If something is bought and not used, that's waste. If it is purchased and not needed, that's money that could have been put to better use. Stories abound from people who, on their own for the first time, earning what initially seemed to be an incredible amount of money, quickly got themselves deep in debt. Or they have to cut back sharply on necessities because they have succumbed to the urge to splurge. (See Chapter 4 on managing money.)

SHOP AROUND AND COMPARE

Granted, this is time consuming, but time spent now will reap big benefits in the long run; you'll establish good shopping habits and learn important information about buying. Shopping around simply means making comparisons in costs, quality, styles, advantages and disadvantages. Compare service contracts and warranties as well.

Short of running around from store to store, how does one compare products? Fortunately, there are a number of sources for product comparison. For one, read the trade journals. *Road & Track* or *Car and Driver* for cars, for instance. *Personal Computing* reviews home computers regularly, evaluates new components and gives the pros and cons of each.

The Better Business Bureau has put out a good book titled *Getting More for Your Money*. It covers everything from advertising to water-conditioning equipment and includes calculators, cosmetics, jewelry, legal services, mail order products and refunds and exchanges, to name just a few subjects. It is published by the Benjamin Company and retails for $7.95 in paperback. The bureau calls it "our official consumer handbook and buying guide."

Consumer Reports publishes monthly and annual product comparisons. The publication takes no advertising and doesn't allow manufacturers to use its material for promotional purposes. It can be considered fairly objective and comprehensive. Both can be found in book stores and in many public libraries. They contain much helpful information.

A third source is newspapers and magazines. Begin now to read the paper, looking for columns that deal with consumer issues or that contain helpful hints for solving everyday problems around the house. Clip these items and start files. Women's magazines contain a wealth of information. Some men's magazines include consumer advice, but often, men have to resort to specialty publications, like *Gentlemen's Quarterly* for apparel and *Skiing* for items related to that favorite winter sport.

Buying a Bed

In Chapter 2, I cautioned against buying a used mattress and box spring. Here is what I think can be done to help find those items.

A bed is one thing that *must* be bought from a reputable dealer. This does *not* mean paying top dollar; one can easily purchase bedding on sale. You will be spending approximately one-third of your life on a mattress, so invest in comfort and support.

Begin by visiting department and furniture stores and talking to salespeople. You'll discover quickly if they are knowledgeable. There are some questions to have in mind when visiting, and if a clear answer isn't forthcoming, find someone who can provide it.

Among the questions a salesperson should be able to answer are:

- What is the difference in quality levels within a brand of mattresses or box springs?
- What are the differences between a foam mattress and one with inner springs?
- What is the basis of support in the mattress?
- Why does a mattress require a box spring?
- What kind of warranty does the product have?

THE BOX SPRING

Start with the box spring. This is a necessity, not a luxury. A good one literally is the foundation to your mattress and provides the essential support. Although it is completely covered, any store worth its reputation will have a cutaway section on display. What you are buying is a number of metal coil springs mounted on a wooden base. The important variables are the number of coils and the gauge of the metal from which they are made. The thicker the gauge and the more coils, the firmer the box spring. The heavier you are, the more firmness you will need.

In old box springs, coils often were not wrapped individually. Today, they usually are. Newer box springs often have squared rather than round coils. Some bedding experts believe these are a better bet because they don't shift as easily as the round ones. So look for wrapped coils and coils that are sturdy to the touch. It is your choice whether they are round or squared off.

THE MATTRESS

The mattress should always be bought in tandem with the box spring. They go together like salt and pepper. Mattresses come in two basic forms, foam rubber and inner spring. Again, get the salesperson to show you the inside of the mattress. A foam mattress is just that, foam. There may be several kinds of foam, with different thickness and different weight. But foam is foam. It may be good for a platform bed or for occasional guests, but for long-term use, you're better off with a good mattress and box spring combination. An inner spring mattress should have springs of steel, like the box spring, but should also have various layers of cushioning. Some are likely to be foam, cotton padding or made of other synthetic material. Above all, the mattress should be smooth, comfortable and provide support for your hips and shoulders. Lie down on it. Give it a try. If it doesn't feel right to you, don't make the purchase, no matter how good the buy.

The cover of the mattress should be of good quality, not flimsy. The quilting should be rounded and well defined. You will want to turn the mattress from time to time, both length-wise and over. So be certain the quilting is uniform and equally defined on both sides.

Get the salesperson to explain the contents. They should be on a printed piece attached to the mattress, but see how much he or she knows. Ask why the elements within are important.

You want facts, not superlatives. Beware of words like "finest," "super," "better" and "added." They are meaningless unless you are comparing the mattress to another. There are also several grades of mattress. Ask about the differences.

Mattresses are warranteed. Ask for the details. If your mattress gets lumpy or springs break under normal use within the warranty period, the manufacturer of any warranteed mattress should give you prorated credit on the cost of a new mattress or box spring. If it is a good mattress in the first place, there should be no trouble. The manufacturer's identification label must be left on the mattress because the manufacturer's representative must check the year of purchase and the style of the mattress. This is so they know how much credit to give you on a replacement.

If you have back problems, consult your physician or chiropractor before buying bedding. They may have some special advice. Most people with back problems require an extrafirm mattress. Extrafirm may seem hard and uncomfortable at first, but most users of the extrafirm variety get used to the difference within two weeks. Extrafirm will cost extra, as well.

How much should you expect to pay for bedding? There is no simple answer. It depends upon the manufacturer, where you buy it, the degree of firmness and whether it is on sale. For example, a twin-size bed made by one major manufacturer and sold through a well-known department store chain was priced recently at $120 for either the box spring or the mattress, $240 for the set. During a sale period, the cost was reduced to $120 for both. A double bed and box spring, somewhat firmer, was priced at $600 regularly and was on sale for $299. A "top of the line" two-piece queen-size bed cost $800 normally and was available on sale for $399.

If you are considering a queen- or king-size bed, make sure that it fits into your abode. A friend bought a king-size bed for a small row home and found that because the box spring didn't bend, he had to remove a window and frame to get the bed into the bedroom. Make sure that once in the room, it doesn't crowd out other essential furnishings, such as a dresser, desk or nightstand.

King-size beds are expensive. They can cost anywhere from $600 to $1,200. By waiting to purchase one on sale, you can save up to 50 percent on some brands.

Bed Linens

Whether you bring your own bed or buy it new, you also will need bedding. If you were fortunate enough to accumulate some, fine; if not, a little information about bedding may be helpful.

SHEETS

Here you have three choices regarding where to purchase: 1) department stores or linen specialty shops, 2) discount stores, 3) factory outlets. You're likely to find a broader selection at the first, lower prices at the second and still lower prices for seconds or irregulars (imperfects) at a factory outlet.

You also have several choices in fiber content. From a cost standpoint, top of the line is 100 percent cotton. Unless it contains some artificial fibers, such as polyester or acrylic, you are likely to have to iron it a little from time to time.

Next is a blend of polyester and cotton. One brand I inspected was conspicuously labled "no-iron" and with a higher percentage of polyester (65 percent) than cotton (35 percent). Other manufacturers offer products that are $^{50}/_{50}$ or $^{60}/_{40}$ percent polyester/cotton.

There are also two kinds of cotton/polyester sheets: percale and muslin. Percale means the fiber count is 180 to 200 threads per inch, while muslin is only 130. The difference, as far as you and I are concerned, is that the muslin sheets feel rougher to the touch, won't wear as well over the long run and are less expensive.

Sheets come in varying sizes, single or twin, full, queen and king. They also come in flat and fitted. Cost increases as the bed gets larger.

Following is a simple chart comparing costs at a department

store, discount store and factory outlet for twin-, full-, queen-
and king-size sheets, regular and on sale.

	Department Store		Discount Store		Outlet	
	Regular	Sale	Regular	Sale	Regular	Sale
All Cotton						
Single/twin	$24	$12	$15	$7.99	not available	
Full	35	17	20	14.95	"	
Queen	47	18	25	17.95	"	
King	60	23	30	21.95	"	
Polyester/Cotton (percale)						
Single/twin	$12	$7.99	$9.99	$6.79	$10.95	$2.99
Full	15	7.99	12.99	8.79	13.95	5.99
Queen	23	9.98	18.99	12.79	16.95	8.99
King	29	12.98	22.99	18.79	16.95	8.99
Polyester/Cotton (muslin)						
Single/twin	not available	$4.97	not available		not available	
Full	"	6.97	"		"	
Queen	"	12.97	"		"	
King	"	14.97	"		"	

BLANKETS

There also are several different options in blankets. Depending
upon the area of the country, personal preferences and the degree of warmth one is seeking, you may choose a lightweight
flannel, heavy wool, electric or a blanket in combination with a
comforter.

The lightest blanket is polyester. It costs less than $10 for a
twin- or full-size and slightly more than $12 for a queen. An
acrylic model, slightly heavier, was available only in full and
queen for $16.97 or $23.97. Neither the department store nor
the discount store had a 100 percent wool or predominantly
wool mixture. However, a catalogue from a major outerwear
company priced a wool blanket at $100. A blend of polyester and
acrylic in an electric blanket was available for $22.88 marked
down from $28.96 at the discount store, and they ran from $49 to

$59 on sale at the department store. Regular prices were from $70 to $100.

COMFORTERS

Ready to spend big bucks? Purchase a goose-down comforter. Regularly $340 and $480 for a twin- or full-size, these were on sale for $199 and $279. However, a comforter made of other materials can be purchased for considerably less. And most comforters double as a bedspread these days. Regular comforters begin at $30 on sale and run up to $200 at regular price, with a full range of fabrics and styles.

SPREADS AND PILLOWS

Spreads cost from as little as $9.97 for a light plaid twin-size to more than $75 for a fine cotton and polyester model with an attractive border and matching flounce.

Pillows come in standard and queen sizes, in a variety of filling materials. The most common is a polyester at $4.77 for standard and $7.47 for queen. It can be easily laundered. Pillows with the same kind of filling at a department store were available regularly for $15 and $17 each and were on sale at two for $13 for either standard or queen. Feather-stuffed pillows weren't available at the discount store, but were on sale at the department store at two for $22, normally priced at $20 and $22 each. A second department store was selling the fiber-filled pillows at $9 each for either standard or queen and the feather-filled pillows for $16 each, regardless of size.

CLOTHING

One theme found throughout this chapter is, "Don't buy it if you don't need it." This especially holds true with buying clothing. Styles, peer pressure and the dictates of certain activities seem to demand a variety of clothing.

Now that you are living independently, clothing needs will change. And if you are living in a strange community away from home and school, so will places to buy clothing. There is no better moment than now to begin to adjust clothing-buying habits.

TAKING STOCK

Start by taking stock. Throw out things you haven't worn in more than a year or that are being kept because someday you'll grow back into them. You probably won't.

Then divide clothes into several categories: work, lounging, dressy, semidressy, leisure and sports. Working in an office, you'll need a certain number of suits, slacks and sport coats, dresses and skirt and blouse or sweater combinations. These will change with the seasons in most parts of the country.

Make a list of items you have in each category. Then determine what is missing. That will help you decide what's needed.

Janice T.: "I spent almost $1,500 for clothing. I had almost nothing I could use in business. My school wardrobe was so different. Now I'm learning to sort out options; to prioritize."

Most important at this juncture should be the clothing worn at work. Unless this is already a familiar atmosphere, some items are most likely to be added.

Figure out what is needed in each category. What is most important? It may be a dress coat for winter or several pairs of dress shoes. Whatever the case, put the list in the order of importance.

COMPARE COSTS

Next, begin to attach some rough prices to each item. Remember that good clothing is an investment, not an expense, and quality items will last. Don't scrimp on things like an overcoat, suits, shoes.

Chris D.: "My advice is to buy as little as you can, but buy quality. Buy stuff to last; suits, skirts and blouses—mix and match. Avoid fads and trendy stuff. Compare prices and watch for sales."

Make comparisons in prices by reviewing catalogues, advertisements from good stores and by visiting department or specialty stores. This should provide a range of costs and some indication of how much will be needed to expand your wardrobe.

You should not have to pay full price for most items. Between discount houses, factory outlets, sales and thrift shops, a good deal of money can be saved on most purchases. Shoes may be the most significant exception, but if you're lucky, even here, savings can be realized. Remember, it is your money, and there is only so much. Make the most of it.

The subjects of how to pick the right clothing, dressing appropriately in business and how to tell quality has been dealt with in a number of books. I recommend one or more of the following if you wish to deal with those aspects in some depth.

- *The Professional Image*, Susan Bixler, G. P. Putnam's Sons.
- *Dress for Success*, John T. Molloy, Warner Books.
- *Woman's Dress for Success*, John T. Molloy, Warner Books.
- *Executive Style; Looking and Living It*, Diana Jewell and Mary B. Fiedorek, New Century.
- *The Consumer's Guide to Menswear*, Donald Dolce, Dodd, Mead.
- *Working Wardrobe*, Janet Wallach, Acropolis Books.
- *Taking Care of Clothes*, Mablen Jones, Eastown Publishing.
- *Cheap Chic*, Caterine Milinare, Harmony Books.

For men, *Gentlemen's Quarterly* or *M* deal with current trends in men's wear. Women can peruse *Glamour, Mademoiselle, Harper's Bazaar, Ms., Working Woman, Savvy* or *Self.*

WHERE TO BUY

Start with specialty clothing stores or department stores. Check out prices and styles. Then try the discount stores or factory outlets. Compare again. The sport coat in the quality store may be available in the right size at the factory outlet for about one-half the price. Then again, it may not. Unlike department or specialty stores, discounters or factory outlets don't always have what you want when you want it. Sometimes a visit will produce treasures and sometimes trash.

Also, when dealing with the discounters and the outlets, don't expect a helpful salesperson to come around. You're on your own. Ask people at the checkout counter if the racks contain any irregulars or seconds (items that were rejected for sale in a standard store because of defects of one kind or another). If the store people assure you that the material is all first quality and consists of overruns and discontinued lines, buy with confidence.

Another place to save, unless you are a purist, is the thrift shop. I know a former stockbroker, a well-dressed individual by anyone's standards, who hasn't purchased a suit or sport jacket in a regular store in years. He haunts hospital thrift shops in quality upper-income communities and finds a wide range of excellent items at bare-bones prices. The rich often donate things to these shops and take tax deductions in return as charitable contributions. A great many items are barely worn, and the labels are some of the finest and best known around.

CLEANING

Now that you are about to invest in some good clothing and know that you are likely to continue that practice in the future, here are a few tips on care of clothing and some idea of what it might cost to repair or alter items.

Suggestions gathered from the Neighborhood Cleaners Association and other sources suggest the following:

1. Read the care label attached to your garments. This will
   provide general guidelines on care.

2. Don't assume that stains removed by water are definitely gone. Many stains are "invisible" initially but show up later, even after dry cleaning. This includes such food stains as fruit juices, alcohol and soft drinks.

3. Fabrics can be discolored or weakened by perspiration, antiperspirants or depilatories. Clothing with these kinds of stains should only be dry cleaned.

4. Dyes used in silks bleed easily. They may also lose color with exposure to sunlight. Silk fabrics degrade in contact with perfumes and deodorants.

5. Do not dry clean imitation leather made of vinyls.

6. Acrylic and polyester materials have a tendency to "pill," or form tiny balls of material, that make a shirt or blouse look "fuzzy." They are difficult to remove.

7. Buttons and beads on regular clothing or coats may bleed. Metal buttons may rust. Some plastic beads or buttons dissolve in dry cleaning fluids.

8. Check to see if belts are marked dry cleanable. Some, particularly on women's dresses and suits, have glued backs that break or come apart in cleaning.

9. Always discuss with the dry cleaner care of items that have not been previously cleaned. Have wearing apparel cleaned as soon as possible after it has been stained. Tell your cleaner what caused the stain so he'll know how to treat it.

Like so many other things, the cost of dry cleaning varies by garment and location. You're likely to pay more in New York, Chicago or Los Angeles than you will in smaller communities, but an average cost range would be:

Man's suit (two pieces)	$4.80
Woman's suit (two pieces)	$6.00
Woman's dress	$5.00
Man's raincoat (rainproof)	$8.50
Man's slacks	$2.40
Skirt, plain	$2.75
Skirt, pleated	$3.50–$6.00
Overcoat	$7.75

REPAIRS

If you need repairs or alterations, your dry cleaner may be able to help. If not, seek out a tailor and obtain price comparisons. Torn seams, for instance, could cost $3 or more; replacing buttons, 25¢ to 50¢ each; hemming, $8 and up, much more if the hem is on a pleated skirt. To take in a skirt waist would cost about $4.50 in many places. Putting cuffs on a man's trousers could be $6 to $10.

Most discount clothing stores do not provide alterations. They may recommend someone who can. Many department stores and men's or women's specialty stores have tailors on the premises. Some provide alterations free with the cost of the item, but always inquire about the cost of alterations.

Telephone Services

The telephone service system as you have known it has changed drastically since January 1984. Once the famed and fabled "Ma Bell," or the Bell Telephone Companies, were owned and operated by American Telephone and Telegraph Company (AT&T). They maintained a virtual monopoly on phone service. Today, AT&T and the Bell System have been broken up, resulting in several major changes in phone service that will affect you.

First, the local phone company will continue to provide service to your home or place of business. But that service stops at the building. Second, the phone, like the variety of electrical appliances in each home, has become a separate entity as far as service goes. Third, the option now exists of buying or renting a phone. The local phone company has eliminated the rental provision, but one can still rent a phone through AT&T. And finally, while you will still pick up the phone to make long distance calls, they will be processed by one of a host of new companies or by AT&T.

Even though your dream apartment may have a phone when you look at it, that phone will not be there at moving time. You will have to buy or rent a phone and plug it in. The local phone company will assign it a number and activate the service.

Buying the Phone. In the past, all home telephones were the property of the phone company, and a customer rented the phone for a monthly charge. Now, as a result of the Bell breakup, most phones will be purchased.

To obtain comparative costs, determine from AT&T the monthly charge to rent each telephone and multiply by the number of months in the year. This determines how much you will pay just for the annual use of that instrument. Now compare this against the amount it will cost to purchase a phone. This will indicate how many months' rental will equal the cost of the phone. In addition to being able to buy a phone from AT&T, virtually every major shopping mall now has a phone store, and many chain stores, such as Radio Shack and K-Mart, sell phones as well.

As is appropriate with any other form of appliance, cost should be measured against quality. Cheap phones will become a throwaway item when it costs more to repair it then to purchase a new one. Check out sound reproduction and the reputation of the manufacturer before purchasing. Some consumer publications are now beginning to evaluate phones. Phones made by Western Electric, formerly a Bell Telephone affiliate, were quality instruments. Can you remember ever having a problem with the phone in your home? If you are confused by the plethora of phones available today, you'll not likely go wrong if you purchase a Western Electric or AT&T product. In any case, examine the phone to see if it has an FCC registration number. This means it is compatible with the phone company's service lines.

If phone service is disrupted at some point, it is imperative that the problem be identified as either the service, the wiring or the instrument itself. If it is the latter, you will have to take it to the repair shop. If it is the service, the phone company will repair it at no cost to you. Some phone companies are offering a monthly maintenance charge for wiring inside your building. This assures that your service will always be promptly repaired if anything goes wrong. You may wish to compare the annual cost of this maintenance fee against the cost of having a repair person come to your dwelling to fix something.

Other phone costs will be incurred for special kinds of phones beyond the standard rotary dial model, such as touch tone, automatic redialing, additional jacks in the wall so the phone can be moved easily from room to room, an unlisted number and extra-long cords. Anything other than a standard phone will cost extra, and you'll be amazed at how quickly extras add up.

Don't be carried away with all the fancy frills some new phones offer. Automatic redialing may be a nifty idea, but employ the rule of thumb, "Do I really need it?" Likewise with portable phones that can be taken to the porch or patio or out on the lawn, within 500, 700 or 1,000 feet from your residence. How often will you need this service? Is it worth the extra cost?

Cost of Phone Service. If a phone is being installed for the first time and you have no, or a very brief, credit history in the community, you probably will be charged a deposit fee up front. The fee, which generally represents an estimation of your bill for one or two months, is similar to the deposit the landlord requested. It can be as much as $100 or more.

Following are examples of charges, including deposits where applicable, for installation of private telephone service in seven cities across the nation, as of March 1984. (Because of the rapidly changing nature of the telecommunications business, these rates may have changed at the time you apply for phone services.)

DALLAS

Deposit: Between $100 and $125
Installation: With a jack—$64
            Without a jack—$91.80
Monthly charges: $15 to $25

DENVER

Deposit: Minimum of $100*
Installation: With a jack—$59.15
            Without a jack—$103.10
Monthly charges: $9.44 for local, unlimited service

*Deposit will be held for one year and will earn 12 percent interest if bills are paid on time.

SEATTLE

Deposit: $80
Installation: With a jack—$27
              Without a jack—$34 (estimated)
Monthly charges: $13.89 (rotary), $14.54 (touch tone) for local, unlimited service

NEW YORK (Manhattan)

Deposit: None if credit is good
         $100 if no credit established
Installation: With a jack—$46
              Without a jack—$94
Monthly charges: $8.13 (individual message rate)

KANSAS CITY

Deposit: $50 and up
Installation: With a jack—$38.40
              Without a jack—$55.45
Monthly charges: $10.70 to $11.70

BALTIMORE

Deposit: $50
Installation: With a jack—$37
              Without a jack—$100 (estimated)
Monthly charges: About $16.49 local, unlimited service

BOSTON

Deposit: None, unless no or bad credit
Installation: With a jack—$32.75
              Without a jack—$62
Monthly charges: $10.60 local, unlimited service

LONG DISTANCE CALLS

The local phone company will no longer process long distance calls as in the past. There are now several choices. The customer still will contact the local phone service to begin a call. But here the process changes. Unless the customer chooses to stick with AT&T's long distance service (that which is in place now), he has the option of calling a local access code or a local phone number to reach an alternative long distance service. Names of long distance providers, like MCI, Sprint and Metrophone, will become increasingly familiar. New legislation passed by Congress has provided these companies with access to all the phones in the country, and they, in turn, provide long distance service in competition with AT&T, often at significantly lower rates.

When calling the local phone company to begin service, the phone company will ask which long distance service is desired. Undoubtedly, the choice will be based on two criteria; cost and where you call most frequently. If calls are to major metropolitan areas, there should be no problems. But if calls generally are to small communities, long distance service may not be available from all companies. It will come, but as of early 1984, the alternative long distance services are still testing their wings. Costs will vary by time of day and day of the week.

If you want to save telephone costs, check with several long distance phone services.

There are several books available that examine the changing telephone scene. It might be worthwhile spending an evening browsing through one or more. You could save a bundle on cost of phone, long distance calls and even installation. Consider:

- *Your Telephone: Operation, Selection and Installation*, Howard W. Sams & Co.
- *The Phone Book*, Larry Kahaner and Alan Green, Penguin.
- *Kiss Ma Bell Goodbye: How to Install Your Own Telephones, Extensions and Accessories*, Wesley Cox, Crown Publishers.

Your Rights as a Consumer

As a consumer, you have numerous rights, such as to:
- expect that the product or service is as advertised;

• expect that the product will perform to the limits of its guarantees or warranty;
• expect that food you purchase is uncontaminated and fit for human consumption;
• know the contents of foods, drugs and cosmetics, to know if they are liable to produce side effects if you use them and what those side effects might be;
• know how much you will have to pay for an item that is financed. This includes the basic cost of the item, the monthly and annual finance charges and the total cost, including financing charges, on both a monthly and a contract term basis;
• know the fiber contents of clothing you buy;
• buy products that are not hazardous to your health or dangerous if properly used;
• examine your credit record or rating at any credit bureau;
• avoid mail solicitations from firms with which you do not wish to do business;
• seek legal or regulatory action against any individual or organization that violates any of your rights as a consumer.

How to Take Action If You Have a Problem

If you believe you have been victimized by a merchant, here is a six-step process for redress of grievance:

1. *Approach the merchant* in a firm but diplomatic manner and present your complaint. If you want the same product but one that works or is in good condition, ask for an exchange. If you want your money back because the product wasn't what it was purported to be or quit working long before it should have, request a refund. Start with the salesperson or store manager.
2. *Write to the company* if you receive no satisfaction. Explain your concern and what you want done. If the letter is not answered within a few weeks or if you receive an unsatisfactory form letter in return, write directly to the president of the company. Include a copy of both the original letter and the form letter or other response.

3. *Contact the Better Business Bureau and the city or state office of consumer protection* if the firm is locally owned and relatively small and you have not received a satisfactory response at this point. Include copies of your correspondence. Let the merchant know in writing what you are doing and why.

4. *Write to the appropriate federal agency* for assistance if the company is national, does business over state lines or is federally regulated (food, drugs, cosmetics, electrical or flammable goods, for instance). (A partial list of these agencies is included at the end of this chapter.) Send copies of correspondence you have initiated prior to contacting the federal agency.

5. *Send a copy of all correspondence to your Congressman or Senator* with a carbon copy to the agency if you do not receive a satisfactory response from the federal agency. This frequently gets rapid results. Congressmen and Senators are there to represent you in exactly this kind of matter.

6. *Consider taking the complaint to the local small claims court* if all other avenues fail and you believe you are in the right. Small claims court is *not* the place to go for federally regulated matters. It is if you feel the landlord is wrong in withholding your security deposit, the TV set bought at a local discount store went on the blink after two weeks and the merchant says "sorry," the cleaners ruined a suit or dress and refuse to reimburse you and so forth.

Call the local consumer protection office (it may be listed under a variety of names) for assistance. If you can't find it, call the local legal services agency and ask them. The consumer protection office will be able to provide step-by-step guidance on how to go about filing a small claims court action. It is not expensive, and an attorney is not necessary.

Make sure facts are straight and that documentation is as thorough as possible. This is vital. Have dates, names and receipts.

Although the whole process may be annoying and time consuming, it can be a terrific learning process, and you may have

the satisfaction of winning if the merchant is really in the wrong.
Most important, it is your right, if you choose to exercise it.

Understanding Warranties

One of your rights as a consumer, and an important one at that,
is to take advantage of the terms of the warranty a manufacturer
provides along with a product. Not all products contain a warranty, but those that do obviously are more appealing to the
buyer. It is assurance by the manufacturer or seller that the
goods or services are as represented or will be as promised. If
you are looking at two toaster ovens alike in all respects, but one
has a warranty and the other doesn't, you obviously would buy
the one with the warranty. The manufacturer, therefore, has a
marketing edge over the competition when it stands behind its
product.

Federal laws require certain things of a warranty. The requirements differ if the warranty is full rather than limited.

A *full warranty* requires the following:

- must be explicit in language and condition of responsibility;
- must state what is *not* covered;
- must be clear if only *some* parts are covered by the warranty
  (engine, transmission and drive train of a car, for instance);
- must clearly state what the buyer must do to take advantage of
  the warranty;
- must state who is responsible for what costs (who pays the
  postage to return the items to the factory, for instance);
- must include a time limit if the product is to be repaired or
  replaced due to something covered by the warranty;

In the case of a full warranty, the seller is obligated to repair
the product promptly, without charge, when notified of its de-
fect. Shipping charges are paid by the seller or manufacturer. If
the product is not satisfactory after a reasonable effort to repair
it, you must receive a full refund or the product must be replaced.

The full warranty must apply to all users, not just the person who purchased the product.

A *limited warranty* must be so labeled prominently and clearly. It differs from a full warranty in that limitations must be spelled out.

In either case, if you are not satisfied with your treatment, you have the right to appeal to the Federal Trade Commission.

IMPLIED WARRANTIES

The federal authorities have taken your consumer rights one step further. Now, products contain an *implied* warranty as well. This simply says that someone selling a product implies that it is as represented, that it should work correctly and last for a reasonable time under normal use. If it doesn't, you may seek satisfaction.

Consumer-Interest Agencies

While most communities have one or more consumer-related agencies and virtually every state has some office, bureau, department or agency that deals with consumer concerns, a great many of the avenues for recourse are federal. Many of these have regional offices that are listed in your phone book. A partial list of the national offices follows:

Office of Consumer Affairs
Washington, DC 20201

Food and Drug Administration
5600 Fishers Lane
Rockville, MD 20852

Federal Trade Commission
Bureau of Consumer Protection
Pennsylvania Ave. at 6th Street, N.W.
Washington, DC 20580

Consumer Product Safety Commission
7215 Wisconsin Ave., N.W.
Washington, DC 20250

Department of Agriculture
14th Street and Independence Ave., S.W.
Washington, DC 20250

Department of Commerce
14th Street and Consititution Ave., S.W.
Washington, DC 20203

You may reach your Congressman or Senator at:

U.S. House of Representatives
Washington, DC 20515

U.S. Senate
Washington, DC 20510

A partial list of state agencies follows:

California:

Department of Consumer Affairs
1020 N. Street
Sacramento, CA 95814

Georgia

Consumer Protection Office
Department of Agriculture
309 Agriculture Building
Capital Square, S.W.
Atlanta, GA 30334

Illinois

Consumer Protection Division
Office of the Attorney General
160 N. LaSalle Street
Chicago, IL 60601

Massachusetts

Executive Office of Consumer Affairs
McCormack State Office Building
1 Ashburton Place
Boston, MA 02108

Minnesota

Office of Consumer Services
Metro Square Building
7th and Robert Streets
St. Paul, MN 55155

New York

Consumer Protection Board
Executive Department
99 Wabash Ave.
Albany, NY 12210

Washington

Consumer Protection Office
Dextor Horton Building
Seattle, WA 98104

If you are interested in pursuing consumer interests on a broader scale, consider affiliating yourself with the Consumer Federation of America. It is found at Suite 406, 1012 14th Street, N.W., Washington DC 20005.

Two consumer rights publications worth exploring are:

- *You and Your Rights*, the editors of *Reader's Digest*, Reader's Digest.
- *The Product Safety Book*, Consumer Federation of America.

Following are a number of the better consumer interest publications I can recommend to you:

- *Dollars and Sense*, by Elizabeth McGough, Wm. Morrow.
- *The Help Book*, by Janet Barkes, Scribners.
- *Guide to Consumer Services*, by the editors of *Consumer Reports*.
- *The Complete Consumer Book*, by Bess Myerson, Simon & Schuster.
- *The Consumer's Handbook*, by Paul Fargis, Hawthorn Books.
- *More for Your Money*, by Mary Bowers Hall, Houghton Mifflin.
- *Guide to Federal Consumer Services*, U.S. Government Printing Office.
- *1984 Consumer Buying Guide*, by the editors of *Consumer Guide Magazine*, Signet.

6

Banking:
Meeting the Money Changers

At this point, most of you will have had some experience with banks. Perhaps you had a checking account in school or deposited money in a small savings account. However, now that you are living independently, it will be worthwhile to understand something about banking beyond those early experiences.

Banking Is Changing

Banking has changed rapidly over the past several years and is continuing to change at an increasing rate. Many of the changes have effected "the little guy," and your banking habits will be different from those of your parents.

In the past, for instance, your primary contact with the bank might have been the friendly teller. Today, banking in most large cities is accomplished with an automatic teller machine (ATM), often after normal banking hours. You may not see a real person for months, and before you know it, especially in cities with extensive cable TV hookups, you'll be doing your banking from home, through a telephone and a TV set. The home banking concept is being tested successfully in a number of American communities right now.

Five years ago, there was no such thing as earning interest on your checking account funds. Now, there are several such options. A few years ago, checking was free at most banks. You had to purchase the checks, but you weren't charged for using them. That concept has gone the way of the dinosaur.

A Tightly Regulated Industry

Banking is tightly regulated. Both state and federal authorities are interested in how bankers take care of your money. Some banks are chartered (given a license to do business) by the federal government. They are known as national banks. You probably have a First National Bank in your hometown. These are part of a large consortium of banks that are members of the Federal Reserve System.

Other banks, largely those that originally planned to stay local in nature or that didn't like the idea of federal regulation, became state-chartered. While many gave up some of the advantages of voluntary membership in the Federal Reserve System, they gained others, primarily their local regulation.

Either way, banks have been rather tightly controlled since the collapse of the banking system in America in 1929. Congress resolved shortly thereafter that the federal government had an obligation to protect depositors. To do this, they created the Federal Deposit Insurance Corporation (FDIC). This independently run, quasi-governmental agency currently insures your deposits in each commercial or mutual savings bank up to $100,000, in the aggregate. A similar service is provided to savings and loan associations and credit unions by parallel agencies.

Congress also passed a massive set of regulations that has governed the banking business for over fifty years. Only recently has the government begun making efforts to deregulate banking.

Different Kinds of Banks

Here's a breakdown of the five kinds of banks that you may encounter.

COMMERCIAL, "FULL SERVICE" BANKS

First, and most common, is the commercial, "full-service" bank. It is so named because it provides a full range of services to both individuals and businesses. It can take in deposits, lend money for a broad range of uses and offer trust services (more about that later). There are approximately 15,000 commercial banks in the United States, in virtually every community. This kind of bank is publicly owned by stockholders who have purchased shares in the company. Deposits are insured by the FDIC.

MUTUAL SAVINGS BANKS

Second is the mutual savings bank. This is a nonprofit institution, owned by its depositors. Until recently, it could not provide checking accounts or loan money for automobiles, boats, commercial ventures, etc. However, that has changed. Today, mutual savings banks are offering checking and some commercial loans. With deregulation efforts underway, they are gearing up to provide everything a full-service bank now offers.

Mutual savings banks operate only in about one-third of the states. Deposits are insured by the FDIC, and its loans are primarily in home mortgages, home improvements and commercial mortgages. The largest institution, in Philadelphia, was seeking to change from a nonprofit, or mutual, status to a profit, or stock, status at the time of this writing. Others were following suit, and a few already have made the change.

SAVINGS AND LOANS

Third is the savings and loan, or building and loan, association. These operate in every state. Some are owned by their depositors, others by stockholders. Like commercial banks, they are either state or federally chartered. Their primary role has been to provide home mortgages and home improvement loans. Regulatory changes are rapidly altering the role and scope of services offered by the so-called S&L. Deposits are insured by the Federal Savings and Loan Insurance Corporation (FSLIC).

PRIVATE BANKS

Fourth, and admittedly rare, is the private bank. This is generally a partnership doing very specialized banking. It takes deposits from anyone, is not insured by the federal insurance organizations, and generally does not make small loans. As one private bank official noted recently, "We don't make loans on Chevys. Perhaps a Jaguar or Mercedes, but not a Chevy." This kind of bank generally pays higher interest than any of the others, but it represents a greater risk.

CREDIT UNIONS

The fifth banking service is provided by credit unions (CU). Credit unions are associations set up by members who represent some sort of homogeneous group. Trade unions often have credit unions for their members. There are some residential credit unions in some major cities. Some companies urge employees to form credit unions, and some professional associations (teachers, for example) have credit unions.

The CU is run by its members on a one-member, one-vote basis. They provide a place to save and make essentially small loans. Some credit unions are financially strong enough to make mortgage loans as well. Many now offer a full bag of tricks, providing competition for the full-service banks. Some CUs offer members such extras as consumer protection information, discounts on various purchases and group insurance coverage. Deposits are insured up to $100,000 by the National Credit Union Administration, in most cases. Some are insured privately or by the state.

Banking Now

What should you know about banking as you are setting up housekeeping?

First, find out what kind of banking services are available. Determine your immediate needs. Tuck away for later reference what you may need at some future point. Then ascertain the cost of all necessary services. Contrary to popular belief, all banks aren't the same. Some banks charge more for services; others pay higher interest on savings. Comparison shop!

Research shows that most people choose their bank because of convenience. That used to mean living or working near the bank. But convenience today may mean how many ATMs they have, the number of drive-in windows, whether one can bank by mail, funds can be transferred by telephone or bills paid by phone. Proximity is no longer as important.

So, pick two or three banks, especially those with ATMs, and begin to compare services.

Checking

Let's start with checking. Today, virtually every household has a checking account. But as you may have discovered already, requesting checking account information can produce a confusing set of alternatives.

Mylene T.: "When I first arrived here, I had a check for $600 and $200 in cash. When I went to the bank to open a checking account, they requested references from a former employer. I couldn't believe it. I was a student for the past few years, and my employers were all part-time. I found out it would take eight days for my check to clear so I could use the money. And then they wouldn't give me any checks to use. They would mail them to me. But what was I to do in the meantime?"

In most communities, especially large cities, when you apply for a checking account you may have to wait as much as a week to ten days for your checks to arrive in the mail. This is because the bank is protecting itself against fraudulent activity wherein someone opens a checking account with a sizable sum, writes numerous or sizable checks far in excess of the amount in the account and then disappears. This happens much more often than most banks admit.

So, to protect themselves, banks deliver checks to your residence (verifying that you *have* a residence) before permitting you to use them. The delay also allows any checks you may have deposited in opening the account to clear and funds to be in account before a check is written.

To avoid being without money, buy enough traveler's checks to tide you over. That way, you avoid carrying cash, can use the traveler's checks almost anywhere and avoid the hassle of the delay.

Regular Checking

The simplest option is a regular checking account. With it, you pay a small charge for each check written. If you write only a few checks per month, this may be the most attractive option. You will always know the cost of the account.

Few banks provide free checks to customers. Most will try to sell you attractive "designer" checks containing, perhaps, your initials, western scenes, flowers or animals. The array is seemingly endless. The cost is higher than for the plain checks, but this may not be brought to your attention. In some cases, the plain checks will be available—if you ask for them.

"Special" Checking

Next is a "special" checking account. This requires you to keep a certain balance in the account at all times. This amount can run from $100 to $500, but it guarantees "free" checking. The word "free" is in quotation marks because it isn't really free, of course. The bank is investing your money, both the amount you are required to keep as a balance and the rest of your checking funds. And they are earning a modest amount of interest. It is their hope that the cost of the account to the bank is offset by the interest they make on your money.

A variation on this approach is the checking account that requires a certain balance in a *savings* account rather than a checking account. If your funds in the savings account drop below a certain level, you are charged.

NOW ACCOUNTS

A more recent variation is what is referred to as a NOW account. The name NOW has nothing to do with immediacy. It originated with efforts by savings banks and savings and loans to enter the checking arena. The vehicle these institutions used was called a Negotiable Order of Withdrawal. Hence the term NOW account.

Commercial banks soon followed suit and offered an account that tied checking and savings together (paying 5¼ percent at this writing) with no money kept in checking. Funds automatically were transferred from savings to checking, and the check was paid. Your checking balance returned to zero until the next transfer. Today, most banks offer some form of interest-paying checking.

"SUPER NOW" ACCOUNTS

More recent still, banks, with permission of the federal regulatory agencies, have begun to offer what they call a "Super NOW" account. This is simply a variation on the regular NOW. The Super NOW pays a rate of interest generally comparable to that earned on certificates of deposit (CD). Certificates require funds to be tied up for varying periods of time, from six months to ten years, for example. The hitch: Super NOW requires a minimum balance of $2,500 to earn the higher interest rate. So, in effect, by having to maintain the $2,500 balance, you still are required to maintain the funds on deposit for long periods of time to earn the higher rate. If your balance drops below $2,500, the money earns a lesser percentage of interest.

Ask your bank's customer service representative to explain the various checking options—regular, special, NOW and Super NOW. Study each carefully to determine which is best for you.

TRANSACTION ACCOUNTS

The newest approach to checking is called by some the "transaction account." Here, all your funds earn interest, and no minimum balance is required in the account. However, although interest is earned on every penny, charges are levied for every transaction—deposits, withdrawals, transfers, by check or by ATM, for the checks you use, for service charges, etc. At the end of the month, the bank adds up all the charges and compares them against the interest the account earned that month. If the interest is higher than the charges, you get the difference. If charges exceed interest, you are charged that amount. Although this can be a complicated accounting process, it is probably a fair banking approach. Most of us give up old habits slowly, and transaction accounts have not caught on quickly, but they may be the way of the future.

SERVICE CHARGES

Service charges can kill you financially. Ask your bank representative to give you a list of service charges and explain each.

Bouncing a check, for instance, can cost you as much as $30. If you are having trouble balancing your checkbook, seeking help from the customer service representative could cost $15 an hour. (There is a way to protect yourself against costly overdraft charges. See page *137* of this chapter.)

Karen C.: "Once, I entered the amount of my paycheck twice in my checkbook. I thought I had more money than I really did and I wrote several checks that bounced. The notice was sent to my parents' home since I hadn't changed my address. By the time I found out the checks had bounced, they had been returned to the places I had paid and resubmitted. Well, they bounced again. By the time I figured out what was happening, the overdraft charges had reached $90. I went into the bank and explained what had happened. They eventually settled for only $30 in overdraft charges. I can't afford to do that very often."

Say you've purchased a product, paid for it by check and that evening found it to be defective. You aren't certain that the merchant will be responsive to your complaint and refund your money. So, you stop payment on the check by notifying the bank. At one bank, this will cost you $8.50.

If proof is needed that you paid for something by check, you can get a copy of the check—for a fee. And so it goes. Charges for special services can be costly. Find out about them ahead of time.

Savings

Saving used to be simple, too. For years, one could go into a bank, inquire about savings rates and be told that the lowest rate was for passbook savings, which allowed money to be withdrawn at any time. The highest rates were for funds left with the bank for several years in the form of certificates of deposit. In between, there were a number of CD options. You could keep funds tied up for from six months to ten years. The longer the commitment, the higher the rate. And if money was taken out early, you paid a stiff penalty.

Well, to some degree you still can do all this, particularly in smaller communities. But savings options have become more confusing as well. This is largely a result of deregulation. The feds have continued to allow banks more freedom in the amount of interest they pay for different time periods. Rates can change weekly. This has made the entire savings business more competitive.

In the late '70s, a whole new financial service was spawned. It was called the money market fund. Nonbanking institutions began offering high interest rates for deposits of as little as $500. A credit card was provided with borrowing levels akin to your amount in the money market fund. You were also granted a checking privilege (actually a Negotiable Order of Withdrawal) and the interest paid changed regularly according to the rates of U.S. Treasury bills. This exciting new product made the banks, with their old hidebound certificates of deposit, look pretty outdated. Regulations prohibited banks from offering a comparable account. So the money market fund people cleaned up, siphoning off billions of dollars from bank savings accounts.

In late 1982, the federal regulators eased restrictions and permitted the introduction of money market deposit accounts, as the bank's answer to the money market funds. In fact, many banks began to refer to their new product as a money market product. It is simply a statement savings account (see below) that pays an interest rate comparable with money market funds. For this product you are required to maintain a $2,500 balance. To obtain funds from the account, you can make a withdrawal at the teller window or, if you have accepted the checking tie in, simply write a check. Some banks have tied a checking account to the money market deposit account and transfer money from savings to checking automatically as the check is presented for payment.

Another savings product worth mentioning was introduced in the mid-to-late '70s. It is called a statement savings account. This emerged because banks found the passbook an expensive item from an operational standpoint. To reduce the high cost of processing deposits and withdrawals, they introduced a new account that, in some cases, does away with the passbook, pays a slightly higher rate of interest and can be accessed on ATMs. Transactions are detailed to the customer in an extensive, computer-produced monthly statement. To many customers, statement savings have become a way of life. And the passbook is no longer offered at many banks.

Uni-Statements

Another customer convenience, developed in the late '70s, is the uni-statement, the single-statement or the all-purpose statement. By whatever name, it combines a number of accounts on one monthly form. Your checking, statement savings, certificates of deposit, automatic payments, bills paid by phone, ATM withdrawals are all included, along with interest paid and service charges rendered. Visa and MasterCard balances are provided as an accommodation by some banks, even though the customer continues to receive a separate monthly statement from either or both.

Customer Service Centers

As banking has become more complex and as changes have become more rapid, many banks have developed a pool of employees called a customer service center or customer information center. This is reached through local or toll-free 800 telephone numbers and provides you, the customer, with access to your accounts via the customer service representative. This individual sits at a computer terminal where he or she can examine your various accounts. In most cases, he or she will be able to answer almost any question regarding your accounts. If not, someone who can help will return your call. Generally there is no charge for this service.

Automatic Teller Machines

Some people think the ATM is the greatest thing to come along since talking movies. Others are scared to death of it. While it is not foolproof, the automatic teller machine has proven to be a boon for countless numbers of people.

It is open twenty four hours a day (except when it is closed for repairs or refill), including nights, weekends and holidays.

Many banks have chosen to put ATMs in places of high traffic for your convenience. Shopping centers are a prime location. The shopping center purported to be the largest in the world, in King of Prussia, Pennsylvania, outside Philadelphia, has no less than five automatic tellers to serve shoppers. One bank has two ATMs within the center and a third at a branch on the edge of the parking lot.

ATMs are simple to operate. They have a keyboard similar to a pushbutton phone, directions are provided on a tiny screen and you are allowed to make mistakes or change your mind in mid transaction . . . up to a point.

You may make deposits, withdrawals, transfers from savings to checking and vice versa, make payments to loan accounts at the bank and pay or withdraw funds from credit card accounts. Depending on the make of the machine or the policy of the bank, other services may be provided. Many banks estimate that as much as 85 percent of the average customer's banking transactions can be done on an ATM.

Marty H.: "I work odd hours and am on the road a lot. Banking during normal hours has always been a problem. With the automatic teller machines I can bank whenever I want, and that has been a help. Last week, I had to be at a meeting in the city at 8:30 and found I didn't have enough money to even park the car. I stopped at my bank's automatic teller on the way in and got what I needed. I don't know what I did before these things were available."

Are ATMs safe? Yes. However, you should use the same precautions when banking at an ATM as when using a conventional bank. Don't flash your money around. Don't use the machine if suspicious characters are loitering nearby or when there are no other people around. To activate the ATM, you need a plastic card and a secret personal identification number. If someone steals your card and tries to use it with the wrong number, the machine will keep the card. So never, but never, put your secret code number on the card. No one can use the card if they don't know your code number.

Obtaining Credit

The Equal Credit Opportunity Act of 1974 guarantees that credit cannot be denied because of sex, marital status, age, race or religion. You also cannot be discriminated against if you are receiving public assistance income or if you have ever entered into a law suit against a creditor.

This does not mean, however, that everyone automatically is eligible for credit. Most companies granting credit will look for criteria. First, the ability to repay the debt; second, the actual payment of past debts.

Your assessesment of ability to pay bills may differ from the creditor's. Creditors establish a minimum acceptable income, and if they feel your expenditures for rent, car purchase, etc. are insufficient, credit will be denied.

Someone who has never had credit has no credit record. Telling a potential creditor that you always paid cash in the past cuts no ice. He or she simply wants to know if you paid your charge accounts or loans on time.

Getting credit is a little like applying for a job. Many employers will not hire you unless you have experience. But how do you get experience? Similarly, many creditors will not grant credit unless you already have it elsewhere.

One way to begin establishing credit is through your local bank manager. After you've been employed for six months or more, ask him or her to suggest ways of establishing a credit rating in your community. The banker may recommend a bank credit card at the lowest level of credit, say $500. Immediately borrow several hundred dollars, put it in a savings account for several weeks and then pay it back. Next month, do the same thing.

Another way to establish credit is by paying back a student loan. If you have had one before, you are required to make payments. Six months of early payments will provide a head start on establishing credit.

A third method is to get someone who already has a satisfactory credit rating (a parent, sibling, etc.) to cosign an application for credit. This means they agree to accept responsibility for your liabilities should you not be able to make payments. Once you've established a payment record, and with the permission of the creditor, the cosigner can be relieved of responsibility and taken off the loan form.

Strangely enough, in establishing credit, it is sometimes easier to get an automobile loan than a credit card. This is because the bank actually owns the automobile until you have paid for it. They can reclaim it if payments aren't made. Buying a car and making regular payments will establish a credit record that the bank will recognize when considering your request for additional credit.

Beyond your ability and willingness to pay, as demonstrated by your past record, the bank may look at your character and financial resources.

Character includes integrity, honesty, trustworthiness and sense of responsibility. These are judgment decisions made by the person taking or reviewing the application for credit. So, if you appear in person to apply for credit, be sure to dress well, be generally conservative in your demeanor and emphasize those things in your background that might help establish your good character. Also try to stress stability. If you have jumped from job to job or residence to residence, have had periods where you were unemployed and doing nothing, if you show up at the bank in unprofessional attire, you will present a negative impression.

Financial resources includes any stock accumulated for or by you, a trust fund left by your grandparents, an automobile you own. Do you have a savings account somewhere? Do you own anything of value, such as a coin collection or an expensive musical instrument? Do you have cash value in life insurance? These are all assets that represent capital to the lender and will help obtain credit.

The Cost of Using Credit

The credit agreement you sign is difficult for most people to understand. Ask the company from whom you are requesting credit to supply information on finance charges and payback periods. They are required by law to do so and to give at least thirty days notice if they change any of the provisions of the contract.

Once a credit record has been created and you are interested in obtaining a loan, shop around. At one bank there was a difference of several percentage points between an interest rate charged on an installment loan for $2,000 and a cash advance on a Visa card for the same amount. At this bank, the Visa advance was cheaper. Further, if you wanted to borrow $3,000 for a year, the rate was 3 percentage points *less* than if you wanted to borrow $2,500. This is not true at all banks and rates will vary widely. So, before you borrow money, check around to obtain the best rate.

A few thoughts to summarize this section:

- *Be aware that credit is costly.* Know what you'll pay for it.
- *If you need money, consider borrowing from your credit union, if you have one, your life insurance* (see Chapter 7) *or the cash option of your Visa or MasterCard.*
- *Understand the details of your credit agreement.* Get copies of the Equal Credit Act of 1974 and of your state's credit legislation from the library and read them. It's your money; you've worked hard to get it. Now protect it.

If you want to know more about credit or are having credit problems, write the National Foundation for Consumer Credit, Inc., 1819 H Street, Washington, DC 20006 or contact your local consumer credit counseling service.

Overdrafts (Bouncing a Check)

If a check bounces, several things happen. First, it goes on your record at the bank. Banks look askance at this sort of thing, and it doesn't look good when you apply for credit. Even if it was a mistake or the result of a mathematical error, the reason is not reflected on the bank's records.

Second, you'll be charged anywhere from a few dollars to $30 or more for each bounced check.

Overdrafts can be avoided at most banks. If you are playing your finances pretty close to the vest, investigate overdraft protection. Here the bank automatically transfers money from a savings account into the checking account to cover the overdraft. There usually is a small charge for the service, but nothing like the charge for a bounced check. You also lose some interest payment.

Another version of this service taps into your Visa or Master-Card. This produces an automatic loan. Some banks will transfer the actual amount needed, and others will transfer in increments of $50 or $100. You will pay interest on the amount transferred.

Special Services

Banks generally have a whole host of special services. Most also won't bring these services to your attention at the time you open a new checking or savings account. You'll have to ask about them. Following is a brief discussion of several of the more important.

SAFE DEPOSIT BOXES

The availability of safe deposit boxes varies from branch office to branch office. Some will have no boxes available, and others will be offering them free for a year just to get potential customers. Check around. Since boxes can cost from $5 to $50 dollars, depending upon bank and size of box, it is worth comparison shopping.

Safe deposit boxes are an ideal place to store valuable records, like insurance policies, birth certificates and passports. Not only are they secure here, but you will know where they are when you want them.

WIRE TRANSFER

David C.: "The first time I learned about wire transfer was when I needed some money from my parents on fairly short notice. My dad reasoned mailing a personal check would take several days to reach me, then take several days to clear at my bank before the funds became available. So he simply arranged for a telegraphing of the money from his bank to mine, and I had it available the next day. That really was an expedient way to do it."

Wire transfer (the sending of funds by telegraph or telephone) isn't something that is used often, but you should know what it is and that it is available. I once came close to running out of money while traveling in England. I went to a local bank, explained my predicament, gave them certain information regarding my accounts at home and whom to contact at the bank. They arranged a wire transfer from my savings account in the United States to the bank in England. If I hadn't known about wire transfer, I don't know what I would have done.

TELEPHINE BILL PAYING

This service, available under several similar names, is gaining in popularity. It allows you to call a special telephone number, often one that's toll-free, and pay your regular bills simply, quickly and without having to write checks. It can be an enormous relief from the frustration of sorting out bill stubs, finding envelopes and stamps and rushing off to the post office in bad weather. The main disadvantage is that the time between your call and the point where the payment is credited on the books of the company you are paying can be several days longer than if you pay by writing a check. This could amount to as much as eight to ten working days and may cause you to miss payment deadlines, incur penalties and create a record of late payments. The service is a good one if your payment order is handled promptly by the bank.

DIRECT PAYROLL DEPOSIT

This service is created by an employer. Here, your payroll funds are automatically deposited as cash into your account. You no longer have to make a trip to the bank on payday. Most banks are now able to make payroll deposits to any bank the employee requests.

CLUB ACCOUNTS

Club accounts—Christmas clubs, vacation clubs, all-purpose clubs—seem to be losing popularity. This may be because they are costly to maintain, and many banks pay little or no interest on them. Here you get a coupon book or a passbook and are expected to deposit a predetermined amount every week or two with the intention of building a specific fund during a specified time period. The bank then sends you a check for the amount saved, with any interest accumulated. It is, nonetheless, a disciplined, forced savings for large expense items, like Christmas, a vacation, taxes, special education expenses, etc.

TRAVELER'S CHECKS

While the competition among agencies, banks, American Express and others is fierce, traveler's checks are most easily obtained through your bank. Many banks provide them free if you are a good customer. Others charge a fee, often $1 per $100 in checks. The seller collects a small fee from you, gets a commission from American Express, Bank of America, Barclays, Citibank, Cooks or a host of other purveyors of traveler's checks, and you go on your merry way. The bank whose name is on the check gets to use your money until the checks clear. I know people who keep a traveler's check or two in their purse or wallets as "mad money" or emergency funds, year after year. In the meantime, some bank is using their funds to invest and earn interest. You get peace of mind, but no interest.

TRUST SERVICES

Many commercial banks have the words "and Trust" attached to their names. In some cases, the title "bank" is left off altogether. There is Wilmington Trust in Delaware, Harris Trust in Chicago and Community Bank and Trust of Denver, for instance.

Trust services are essentially asset management services. The trust department of a bank is designed to manage funds entrusted to it by customers. Sometimes, those funds are from the estate of someone who died and are managed for the benefit of the heirs. Sometimes an individual has funds he or she has neither the time, interest or expertise to manage. These funds will be put "in trust" at the bank, and the bank's trust people will manage the funds, compute and file income tax returns and do whatever else needs to be done to assure the customer of income and financial soundness. The bank therefore becomes the manager of real estate, the investor in stocks and bonds, the disposer of property and agent for a host of other things.

DISCOUNT BROKERAGE SERVICES

Recently, many banks have begun to provide discount investment services to customers, through the trust department. People wishing to make their own investment decisions relative to the purchase of stocks and bonds, rather than going to a recognized stock brokerage firm, now can do so through a bank's discount brokerage service, and save from 15 to 70 percent on the cost of transactions. However, by law, banks are not allowed to offer investment advice to their customers, so don't expect to find an advisor assigned to your account who will call with hot stock tips. You can save money on transactions, but you will have to make the decisions yourself.

Banking is a highly complex industry. It is changing all the time. You are well advised to find yourself a bank branch manager or officer you like and trust. Keep in regular contact with him or her to discover new products and services that are being offered.

For more detailed information on banking, on credit and on

your rights as a consumer from a banking standpoint, you may wish to consult:

• National Foundation for Consumer Credit
1819 H Street, N.W.
Washington DC 20006
• *What Everyone Should Know About Credit*, Editors of *U.S. News and World Report*, Money Manager's Library.
• *All You Need to Know About Banks*, by John A. Cook and Robert Wool, Bantam Books.
• *The Bankers*, by Martin Mayer, Ballantine.
• *Glossary of Banking Terminology*, Running Press.
• *Sylvia Porter's Money Book*, Sylvia Porter, Avon.
• *Everybody's Money Book*, Jane Bryant Quinn, Delacorte.
(Ms. Porter and Ms. Quinn are nationally syndicated columnists who often write about banking and credit.)

7

Insurance: Protecting What's Yours

Sooner or later, you will encounter the strange and often complex world of insurance. It's one of those services classified as "something everyone needs and no one wants." Insurance salespeople have been the butt of jokes for generations. But the concept of insurance dates back well beyond 2,000 years, and not only has it lasted, but it has prospered over time. It is a subject to which some thought should be given because it will confront you regularly in the months and years ahead.

Why You Need Insurance

The basic purpose of insurance is protection against financial loss. At this point you logically may say, "But I don't have anything to lose. I'm just starting out, and not only don't I have any money, I'm in debt."

That may be true. However, I didn't say insurance is protection "for you" against financial loss. It may be, but at this stage in your life, it may also protect your family—parents and siblings—against financial loss that you may create for them.

Let's examine a few simple examples. Suppose you slid off the road in the family car and injured yourself so that you couldn't work for a year. Medical insurance, through your employer, may cover your hospital fees, buy you could lose your job or at least your paycheck. Few employers will continue to pay wages month after month if you are not working. Who pays your student loan? Can you get out of your lease? What about other expenses? Can you move back home? If you have insurance to cover loss of income through accident or serious illness, money will become available to pay for your monthly expenses. The financial responsibility will not fall upon your parents or other relatives. Technically, if you are over twenty one, they have no legal responsibility for your financial burdens, although they may feel they have a moral obligation.

Let's say you've had a small group of people in on a Saturday evening. At 2:00 A.M., you say goodnight to your last guest and clean up the apartment. You empty the ashtrays into a wastebasket, lock the door, turn out the lights and go to bed. At 4:00 you're awakened by the smell of smoke and the buzz of the smoke detector. Embers from a cigarette have set the contents of the wastebasket on fire, and it has spread.

Two hours later, the fire department has everything under control. The tenants of your building are huddled together in the street awaiting permission to return to their apartments. Yours is uninhabitable. Water, fire and smoke have ruined your furnishings, stereo, TV set and much of your clothing.

What will it cost you to find a new apartment immediately? What will it cost to replace the stereo, TV and the hodgepodge of furniture you've acquired? And what about your clothes, skis, tennis gear, or musical instrument? Will the landlord let you out of your lease? Who pays for the damage to your apartment and that of others? Will your boss pay your salary while you take time off to put your life in order?

The answers to these questions vary according to the circumstances. Insurance is the one constant.

If you are attempting to establish true independence, you will not want to rely upon your parents or other relatives. So begin by protecting yourself, and them, against financial loss. You can do this by purchasing various forms of insurance.

What kinds should you consider? How do you determine the amount of coverage? How much will it cost you? Against what kind of financial losses should protection be purchased? These questions and others will be discussed in this chapter. Knowing something about insurance before you are confronted by an agent will be beneficial.

What Is Insurance?

An insurance policy is a legal document. In it, the company states that it is prepared to protect you or those you may injure from financial loss. In return, you agree to pay a certain amount of money to the company on a regular basis. Insurance policies differ, however. One policy may provide more or less coverage than another for the same amount of money. So it pays to compare.

The basis of insurance is sharing the risk of loss. Insurance is based on complex mathematical tables that provide the insurance company with important statistics needed to help determine the cost of their policies. Insurers try to write enough business to accurately predict their losses.

For example, by estimating how many people die each year in different age groups, they are able to predict how many of their customers are likely to die and what amount they will have to pay the estate of those insured. This statistic helps insurers determine the cost for all their policies.

When buying insurance, you pay a certain, relatively small sum of money on a regular basis to assure that you don't have to pay a large amount of money at some unforeseen point in the future.

Insurance, like banking, is a tightly regulated industry. An insurance company must meet certain requirements to be permitted to do business in each state. Insurance agents and brokers must take a test administered by the state and be licensed. This is for your protection. Likewise, insurance advertising is carefully reviewed to assure that no advertising or promotional materials are false or misleading.

What Kinds of Insurance Should You Consider?

There are essentially six forms of insurance you should be aware of: automobile, tenant's, or renter's (often known as a form of homeowner's insurance), liability, medical, disability income and life.

The two most important assets you have are your health and your ability to earn income. Insurance is designed to help you avoid potentially significant financial problems connected with medical costs and loss of income due to illness, accident or death or a liability judgment against you. This would arise through the destruction of property and injury to another person, whether involuntary or voluntary.

AUTOMOBILE INSURANCE

The type of insurance you are likely to encounter first is automobile insurance. It is also one of the more complicated and controversial forms of insurance. In about half the states, the owner of a motor vehicle is required to have automobile insurance. Other states require that he or she demonstrate "financial responsibility."

In addition to determining insurance cost by estimating how many accidents will occur and what the average cost of the accident will be, auto insurers also examine factors such as age, sex, marital status and where you live. For instance, they have determined that people under twenty five are involved in more accidents than people in other age categories. Therefore, these people are charged higher rates.

There are a great number of variables relating to auto insurance. Costs will differ widely. It pays to shop and compare, even though it may be time consuming and confusing. Plan ahead;

check out auto insurance coverages and costs well in advance. Determine the year, make, model and the horsepower of your car's engine. Then begin shopping for insurance coverage.

One very important factor of cost is where the car is registered. Coverage for automobiles housed and registered in large cities could be several times more expensive than the same insurance in distant suburbs or small towns. This is because insurance industry statistics show there are more accidents involving cars garaged in heavily trafficked areas, and the cost of repairing these cars is generally higher.

On the average, commuting to the city from a suburb every day puts more miles on your car than traveling to a job in another nearby suburb. The chances of an accident are greater, because you're driving more miles.

Another factor is horsepower. Insurance on a 350-horsepower Oldsmobile will cost more than a 90-horsepower Volkswagen, for instance. The theory here is that a large, heavy car that demands the higher horsepower can go faster, takes more time and space to stop in an emergency and will strike another object with greater force, thereby doing more damage.

Women generally are considered better risks than men, at least in early age classifications. In some states, the gender differential is being or has been challenged, and rates for men and women of the same age now are the same, all other considerations being equal.

Under certain circumstances you may be eligible to receive a reduction in your rates, for instance, if you have had high grades in school or you own a compact car rather than a midsize or full-size car. Automobiles with some form of passive restraint system, such as automatic seat belts, also may justify some rate reductions.

If you are about to buy a car, check its classifications for insurance purposes. A reduction in auto insurance premiums each year could amount to the cost of a four-speaker car stereo system rather than a plain AM radio, and then some. It can be a significant difference! Your insurance representative will be happy to detail which cars warrant reduced premium rates.

When you move, notify your auto insurer. If you have been

living in an area where rates are high and you move to a lower-rated community, you will receive a reduction in premium. On the other hand, the premium may increase if the reverse occurs. A few words of caution: If you move and don't notify your insurer and subsequently have an accident and file a claim, the insurer *could* void the policy because the information on which the policy was written was incorrect at the time of the accident. More likely, you would be retroactively charged the increased premium for the time you lived at the new address. For that matter, any changes in use, job, the number of people who drive the car and whether it is used for work or pleasure should be reported immediately.

ASSIGNED RISK PLANS

If you have a bad driving record or appear by your age, occupation or education to be a potentially bad risk, you may have trouble getting insurance.

However, you cannot be denied insurance if you are licensed. Most states have developed what frequently is called an assigned risk plan. If someone has been turned down for auto insurance through regular channels, they may apply through the plan. They will be assigned to an insurer, who is selected on a rotation basis. The insurer must accept them as a customer, and they will be serviced the same as any other customer.

The assigned risk plan concept varies in some states. In Maryland, for instance, this kind of business is handled through the Maryland Auto Insurance Fund. In other states, the program is called the Joint Underwriting Association. Still another variation is to have a company accept the questionable risk and then "reinsure" it through what is called a reinsurance facility. Losses suffered by one insurer are shared by all insurers. You and I, as good drivers and good customers, are, in effect, subsidizing the driver who is considered a poor risk.

WHAT AM I BUYING?

When buying automobile insurance, one actually is purchasing several kinds of coverage in one policy. First is *liability* coverage. This offers protection from financial loss if damage has been caused to *someone else's* car, property or person. Payment is for the insurance company's services in defending lawsuits of any kind that allege you caused the damage and payment of any judgment against you (up to legal policy limits).

Suppose you are driving along and swerve to miss an animal, running another car off the road. The other car is damaged, the occupants are slightly injured and they and the car end up in someone else's front yard. Your insurer will defend you in lawsuits that might be filed by the owner of the property whose lawn was damaged. If the suit is lost, your insurer will pay up to the amounts specified in the policy.

When obtaining insurance, determine the monetary limits of your liability coverage. Your agent can explain the options, but a good bit of advice is not to underinsure in this category. The highest levels of coverage are not that much more expensive and judgments of a million dollars are no longer uncommon.

The second form of coverage is *medical payments*. This covers the medical cost of treating injuries suffered within the monetary limits you have purchased. *Coverage is for yourself and any passengers in your car*, regardless of who caused the injury. If you have medical insurance where you work, high limits on this coverage may not be needed, but you will want to protect your passengers. This kind of coverage is optional but worth having.

The third coverage, *collision*, may be purchased or rejected if your auto is owned outright. But if it is being financed, the bank or other financing agency may require it. This coverage *protects you against loss through damage to your car*. Collision and liability coverage are the most expensive parts of an auto insurance package. The cost of this coverage can be reduced, however, by agreeing to pay the first $50, $100, $250 or $500 of any damages yourself. This is called a deductible.

Fourth is *comprehensive* coverage. As with collision or medical, you can elect not to take this insurance if you own the car outright. Financing may require it. This protects you against loss through fire, theft, larceny, glass breakage, vandalism, riot and a host of other perils. This section also provides limited funds to rent a car should yours be stolen.

Individual insurance companies may offer one or more minor

coverages, and some states will require no-fault insurance for a modest fee, but essentially, auto insurance provides the above four major forms of coverage.

NO-FAULT AUTO INSURANCE

Conceptually, so-called no-fault insurance is relatively simple. Practically, it is complicated and fragmented in that it differs from state to state, and about half the states do not have it at all.

With no-fault insurance, the injured parties in an auto accident receive prompt payment of their medical expenses, regardless of fault. Under no-fault, injured parties turn to their own insurer or the insurer of the car in which they were riding for coverage of the injuries. In auto accidents, often there are long and costly investigations and legal battles to determine who caused the accident, the idea being that the person at fault (or his/her insurer) should pay the medical costs. Because medical bills are immediate, the no-fault concept seemed to provide a satisfactory answer. The plan, it was reasoned, would also reduce court overload and the added expenses this represented. In no case does no-fault coverage apply to anything but medical expenses. Because of state-by-state variations, check with your insurance representative to determine whether your state has a no-fault plan and, if it does, how it works.

Insurance for Your Apartment

A relatively simple, inexpensive, but often overlooked form of coverage is tenant's, or renter's, insurance. This is referred to by insurers as OH-4. Tenant's insurance is protection against financial loss caused by the destruction of the contents of your apartment, injury to someone visiting your apartment or harm to their property.

If you live in an apartment building, your landlord or the building owner will have some kind of insurance on the building itself. You have the right to inquire about the extent of that protection. Make certain, for instance, that fire insurance covers your apartment. It won't cover the contents. That's your responsibility. If you caused the fire through negligence, you could be held liable for damage to the property of other tenants.

Take a moment or two to survey the contents of your apartment. You'll have a bed, a couple of chairs, perhaps a table. You may have a coffee table or end table. Undoubtedly, you'll have kitchen items. Then there is your stereo and perhaps a TV. Add a lamp or two, a rug, a clock and your clothing and you have more than you thought. Even if the contents are owned jointly by you and a roommate or some items were borrowed, they still have value and would have to be replaced if destroyed.

Tenant's insurance protects you from loss created by a legal liability. Let's say you served alcoholic beverages to a guest in your apartment and that guest had an automobile accident on the way home. The courts could hold you liable for creating the circumstances that caused the accident. Legal liability cases are seldom simple and often costly to defend, even if you are judged innocent.

Further, while friends are in your apartment, they are your responsibility, legally, once they have crossed the threshold of your door. If they trip and break a leg, you could be held liable for negligence because you didn't secure the rug to the floor. Sound funny? It isn't. Your tenant's policy should have medical payments coverage so the injured person doesn't have to sue you. The potential is always there.

There are many variations in tenant's policy coverage. Discuss them fully with your insurance representative.

FILING AUTO OR TENANT'S POLICY CLAIMS

I hope you never have to file an insurance claim. But if you do, there are several guidelines you should follow.

First, obtain and review your policy; you'll be more knowledgeable in dealing with the insurance company. After reviewing the policy, notify your insurance representative.

Next, follow the directions of the agent or broker regarding filing a claim form. An insurance claims representative may inspect the damage him or herself or just send forms to fill out and return or ask you to obtain several estimates for the repair. Remember, these people work for the insurer, not you. Furthermore, they deal with the insurance claims every day and they'll be very familiar with the contents of your policy. If there is a problem settling the claim, you have a right to ask your broker to represent your interests with the claims people.

If you have an automobile accident, it is important to obtain the name, address and phone numbers of occupants in both cars, especially the other driver. Also get the name of his or her insurer and policy number, if possible. Make a diagram of the accident scene and record the time and place accurately. At this time, *do not admit or accept fault*. That is not a matter for your determination. Unless damage to the cars is obviously minor and there are no injuries, call the police and be as cooperative as possible.

If you have to file a claim on a loss that occurred through fire or other damage to your apartment, it is emormously helpful and beneficial to have photographs of the contents of the apartment. This way, you'll know exactly what was there and won't have to guess. You'll also benefit from knowing the cost of various items and when they were purchased.

You probably have insured your belongings on an *actual cash value* basis. This means their worth at the time they were destroyed, not when they were new. If your sofa is ten years old, its value is that of a ten-year-old sofa, not a new one. The insurance company will reimburse you for that amount. If you want to have coverage based on replacement cost, a substantially higher premium will have to be paid.

File your claim as soon after the accident or destruction as possible. Facts will blur as time passes. Many policies require a claim to be filed within a certain time period.

Debbie G.: "My sister had a cracked windshield at one point. She got it fixed, and it cost her about $70. A stone flew up and hit it, I think. Well, she found out months later that the comprehensive coverage on her automobile insurance would have paid for it. But by then, it was too late. She really didn't know what she was covered for."

Don't necessarily accept the claims check as soon as it is presented. On occasion, claims people will take advantage of an emotionally upset person or one in need of funds. They may try to hurry the settlement for a figure less than is really deserved. Most claims people are honest and helpful, but be certain you understand exactly what the insurer is paying for and how they arrived at the value. If you aren't satisfied, don't accept the check or sign the claims-release form.

Medical Insurance

Like automobile and tenant's insurance, health or medical insurance is a virtual necessity. Fortunately, almost all but the lowest level employers have some form of medical coverage these days. But beware; it pays to know the extent of coverage. Avoid being underinsured when you can least afford it. Many doctors and hospitals will not accept patients, even on an emergency basis, when they have no medical insurance. Always carry your medical insurance card in case of an emergency.

There are four basic forms of medical insurance. The first, *hospitalization*, covers expenses incurred during a hospital stay. It is offered by a host of commercial insurers and, in many areas of the country, by Blue Cross. Included in most policies are room and board, general nursing care and miscellaneous supplies, such as thermometers, soap, bandages and dressings, etc. Frequently *not* included in this coverage are medical tests, casts for broken limbs, extraordinary nursing care and drugs, among other things.

If your employer provides a health insurance plan, determine the extent of your hospitalization coverage. Insurers are competing for business and some will be more generous in their benefits than others. Also check on whether you will be required to pay for some of the hospital costs because the policy has a co-pay or deductible clause. Co-pay and deductibles require payment of a certain portion of the costs, usually the first $50, $100, $500 or $1,000. Sometimes the amount is expressed as a percentage of the total cost or a percentage of your wages.

With hospital costs averaging upwards of $280 a day and the

average stay 7.6 days, according to the American Hospital Association, a percentage deduction could be very costly. Don't wait until you are hospitalized to determine the extent of your benefits.

The second part of your basic coverage pays for *physician's expenses*. This generally provides payments for visits to a physician's office or visits from your physician in the hospital or at home. Again, coverage for this part of your plan varies. Know what you can expect.

Some plans have a deductible as well as a co-pay provision. For instance, you may have to pay the first $100 of physician's office visits. Once you reach $101, the insurer will accept billing and begin to make payments. From this point on, however, the insurer may only pay 80 percent of the costs as part of your co-pay plan. If you have three more visits, at $50 per visit, and the insurer pays 80 percent, you would then pay the remaining 20 percent, or $30.

Third is *surgical expense*. Obviously, not every visit to the hospital results in surgery. But when it does, this kind of coverage generally picks up costs for the surgeon, his assistants, the anesthesiologist, use of the operating room and equipment and costs related to the performance of the operation. Some policies also include a number of visits by the surgeon to your hospital room or home. Again, it pays to see what kind of coverage you have before an operation is needed.

Beyond hospital, physicians and surgical coverage, there is what is commonly called *major medical*. Coverage here begins where the others stop. For instance, items not covered by hospitalization—medical tests, costs for broken limbs, extraordinary nursing care, drugs, etc.—would normally be contained in your major medical insurance plan. Most major medical policies use a deductible or co-payment plan. With medical costs skyrocketing, major medical insurance is vital to your economic well being. If it's not provided by your employer, look into purchasing it yourself.

One final word on major medical coverage. Many insurers provide for regular prescription drug purchases on a co-payment basis through major medical. So save those receipts when you get a prescription filled. You never know how many refills will be needed during the year or how many new prescriptions may be required, and they add up quickly. Some major drug chains even provide a computer printout of all your prescriptions, complete with name of doctor. This record is just what the insurer needs and wants.

If your employer doesn't provide medical insurance, either the basic or major medical plans, consider whether it is available through some other group of which you are a member: a labor union, professional society, fraternal group, religious organization. In some cases, if a number of people share some common interest, a group of your own can be formed. Ask potential insurers what qualifies as a group. Group insurance is almost always less expensive than if you are insured individually.

New Twists to Health Coverage

HEALTH MAINTENANCE ORGANIZATION (HMOs)

Currently, more than 11 million people have elected to have their health care needs provided by a health maintenance organization. There are approximately 275 such organizations nationwide. And both the concept and the number of HMOs are growing rapidly. HMOs represent an interesting alternative to standard medical insurance plans.

Basic to the HMO concept is its attempt to treat members before they need hospitalization. They permit as many visits to the physician as are necessary and all hospitalization when needed for one fixed monthly fee. Members must use doctors, hospitals and other medical care providers who are associated with the HMO plan.

In short, it is a prepaid group plan emphasizing preventive medicine. Because the HMO is still a relatively new concept, there are few HMO organizations across the country. Some are still working out the bugs. It isn't for everyone, but HMOs could be the health care wave of the future for the average American. According to an article in the May 1982 issue of *Changing Times* magazine, "In at least six major metropolitan areas—Los Angeles, San Francisco, Sacramento, Seattle, Minneapolis–St. Paul and Honolulu, more than 20 percent of the population are HMO members."

Individuals can join some HMOs, *but in others members must be part of a group plan.* As with Blue Cross, this can be an employer, a fraternal organization, a professional association, etc.

Urgent Care Centers

A new medical facility, similar to a hospital emergency room, is popping up across the nation. It is called an "urgent care center." At this point there are more than 800, and the number is growing. According to one expert in the field, these unique offices, often located in shopping centers, with extended night and weekend hours, will soon replace the old emergency room and provide faster, better and less expensive emergency care.

Life Insurance

The next kind of insurance you should consider is life.

No one likes to admit he or she is going to die, let alone to plan for it. People in their twenties regard their own demise as something eons away. And for most of you, that fact of life *will* be true.

Reasons for Considering Life Insurance

Although, in years past, life insurance primarily provided burial expenses for a husband and perhaps some funds to ease the family's financial burden, today it can be used in more sophisticated and imaginative ways. For some people, it represents a form of forced savings, while at the same time providing the traditional protection. And the beneficiaries of the protection might be your parents or spouse, who might have to shoulder your financial responsibilities should you die.

Another important use of life insurance is to provide a base for a loan at some point, perhaps for a home mortgage, the education of a child or for an emergency. If your life insurance develops a cash value, the value will build over the years and be available either as collateral for a loan from a bank or directly from your insurer, usually at a lower rate.

David J.: "After a couple of years of paying rent, I decided I wanted to buy a small house. I felt renting was throwing money down the drain. But I didn't have enough in savings for a down payment. My father had taken out a life insurance policy on me when I was in high school, and I had forgotten all about it until I finished college. Then he handed it to me and said it was time for me to start paying the premiums. I wasn't sure I even wanted the policy, let alone make the payments. But he persuaded me to keep it. A few years later, I had enough loan value in the policy so that, with my savings and a little help from Dad, I managed to make the down payment on a little house. It isn't much, but it's mine, and every month, I'm increasing my equity instead of losing money."

Although you are healthy now, there is no guarantee you'll remain that way. Taking out a life insurance policy at an early age can help to buy additional insurance as you need it and when you can afford it, later on. You're also likely to pay lower annual premiums over the life of the policy.

But buying life insurance can be confusing. About 1,800 companies sell anywhere from one to thirty life products. There are many variations on the three of four basic policies from which you will have to choose.

Life versus Other Options

There are people who present a case against life insurance and for other uses of your money—stocks, mutual funds, money market funds, bank certificates of deposit, etc., especially if you already have some form of life insurance coverage through your

employer. And they may be right. You will have to decide what
kind of individual you are before making a choice. Are you a
good saver? Do you have financial obligations you don't want to
inflict upon someone else? Do you plan to be married and raise a
family? What is the likelihood that you'll continue working for an
employer who will provide life insurance coverage? Are you
willing and able to set aside money for other forms of investment? Will you be able to accomplish on your own what insurance can provide? Are your current financial obligations too
heavy to permit either insurance or other forms of investment?
Only you know.

You would be well advised to at least look into life insurance
options, if not for now, for a few years down the road. Life
insurance is one of those things that is largely a future consideration for young people in terms of its payoff. But it needs to be a
present consideration to assure that payoff, in whatever form,
later. And today, women have the same reasons to consider life
insurance as men.

Life insurance rates vary. Depending upon your health,
weight, smoking and drinking habits and occupation, you may
find it difficult or very expensive to obtain coverage. If you are 5
foot 6, 230 pounds, a heavy smoker and you work as a chimney
sweep, don't be surprised if the rates are unusually high or you
have trouble obtaining life insurance at all.

Compare costs by requesting from your insurer or the pub-
lisher, a copy of the most recent *20 Year Dividend Comparison
Study on Life Insurance* from Best's Review. A recent issue
compares the performance and costs of life insurance at fifty
companies. This will provide you with the equivalent of the
average yearly payment for a specific amount of insurance. Even
if you can't figure out what all the numbers mean, you'll wow
your insurance person just by asking about it. If he or she
doesn't know what you're talking about, consider finding another representative. Another source of life insurance comparisons is *Consumer Reports*.

Insurance is a complicated business. Make sure you have a
knowledgeable person or persons serving your needs. He or she
may become a lifelong asset—or liability. The choice is yours.

TYPES OF LIFE INSURANCE

Perhaps the most common form of life insurance is called *term insurance*. This is coverage written for a specific period of time—one, five or ten years, generally. It is the kind your employer provides, if he sponsors a group life insurance plan. When purchased as part of a group plan, it is usually the most inexpensive form of life insurance. When purchased by an individual, it is inexpensive in the early years, but the cost increases as a person ages. Payment is for a certain amount of coverage over a specific time period. There is no cash or loan value in term insurance.

The second kind of life insurance is *permanent, or whole life*. For this, premiums usually are paid until you die. Cash values build up, and in later years, the policy may be surrendered to the company and the cash value withdrawn in a lump sum or as a fixed amount each year for the rest of your life. The premium payment will remain the same for the life of the policy.

There are several kinds of whole life policies, but regardless of the option you pick, be aware that some policies are what the industry calls *participating* whole life policies. Essentially, the participating policies return sums referred to as "dividends." In truth, they are not dividends at all. Actually, the company is returning a portion of the premium. The extra premium has been invested and earned interest. The interest is separated from the premium returned, and you are not taxed on it. In a participating policy, the so-called dividends can build to a point where they are sufficient to pay the premium each year, and you no longer have to pay anything for the protection.

The other option, *nonparticipating* whole life, has a lower premium, much closer to what the insurer believes the cost of the program will be. Here, no dividends are returned.

A relatively new form of life insurance is called *universal life*. Here a term policy is tied to an investment fund. It is flexible and its value can increase or decrease, thereby causing your payment to increase or decrease. This policy is not yet available from all major insurers.

Endowment insurance is another form of life insurance, but one not often sold these days. In this, payments are made for a specific period of time—ten, twenty, thirty years or to age sixty-five. Funds accumulated in the policy are paid on a specified date. This has been a popular way of providing for the education of children or for retirement. If you die before the specified payment date, your heirs receive the full amount of the policy.

VARIATIONS ON THE THEME

There are many variations of each form of life insurance. Some policies combine aspects of two or more forms. Some provide extra coverage if you die in an accident. This is called *double indemnity* and generally pays double the face value of the policy, less any money you may have borrowed from the policy's cash value.

Another option provides for payment of the policy premium in the event you are disabled for a specific period. This prevents the policy from expiring and is called a *waiver of premium.*

If you have had a whole life or endowment policy for some time and it has built up some loan value, some policies authorize the automatic borrowing of funds from the cash value of the policy to pay the premium if a payment is missed.

Another form of coverage to consider at some point is *disability income* insurance. This protects against loss of income due to a long-term illness or a serious accident. Depending upon the provisions of the policy, it will pay a percentage of your wages or a flat dollar amount for a specified time—for life, in some cases—after an initial waiting period.

If you were incapacitated in an auto accident—and young people are eight times more likely to be disabled than to die of an illness or accident—your salary or a portion of it would be paid even if you couldn't work. Some employers provide this coverage as a benefit, but it is particularly important for people who are self-employed, such as doctors, dentists, attorneys, salespeople, artists and, yes, even authors.

If you want to find out more about insurance, there are numerous publications and pamphlets available to you at little or no cost. Many state insurance departments have put out insurance buying guides for consumers. Many also compare the track records of various insurers regarding the payment of claims, complaints against them and their solvency. Following are two places to write to find out more about various kinds of insurance.

- Insurance Information Institute
  110 William Street
  NY, NY 10038
- American Council of Life Insurance
  1850 K Street N.W.
  Washington, DC 20006

How to Find an Insurer

To some, this may seem like a silly question. Usually, insurance people find you. Selection of the person or persons who will represent you may be the most important aspect of your insurance plans. Because there are many ways to find an insurance agent or broker, try these steps.

- Divide your insurance needs into property/casualty (auto, liability, tenant's and the like) and life (this would include medical and disability).
- Check into companies that are both reputable and solvent. Talk with friends or family or ask the research librarian at the nearest public library (in most cases) for either *Best's Insurance Reports* or the *Flitcraft Compend,* which rates insurance companies. *Best's* gives each company a letter rating. Look for companies with at least an A rating.
- Once you've determined which companies you might consider, look in the phone book for a representative near you.
- Talk to several agents or brokers. You'll like some and not others. Pick someone with whom you feel comfortable. Many insurance people are working toward or have achieved professional designations that they receive only after passing rigorous examinations. For life insurance, it is CLU, (Char-

tered Life Underwriter). For property/liability insurance, the
designation is CPCU (Chartered Property Casualty Underwriter). A new designation that some life insurance people are
acquiring is ChFC (Chartered Financial Consultant). This requires a thorough knowledge of many forms of investment, not
just life insurance.

I suggest you obtain two representatives: one for life insurance products and a second for property and casualty. Occasionally, you will find someone representing a company that sells all
forms of insurance. He or she will want to handle all your needs.
Stick with the specialists and be careful about putting all your
insurance eggs in one basket. And if you're being pressured,
back away.

8

Eating: In or Out

People living on their own for the first time find eating habits change, often dramatically. And because food can be expensive, it can make a big dent in your budget. Buying, storing and using food wisely can lessen the financial strain, while allowing you to eat well and intelligently.

Now is an ideal time to get your eating act together, while you are making the transition from meals prepared by school cafeterias or at home to managing your own eating habits.

Debbie G.: "When I got out of school, I was eating quantity. It was so easy to get back in line two or three times at school. After being on my own for six or seven months, I changed. I cut down both on costs and weight. Now, I'm eating quality and enjoying it more."

How you approach the subject of eating is as important to survival on your own—because of it's impact on your physical and emotional well-being and on your pocketbook—as furnishing an apartment, and it can be an important aspect of money management.

General Hints

Here are some general hints on eating:

1. Before making dramatic changes in your diet, consult a physician or dentist for some nutrition education.
2. If you choose not to seek out either, consider a trained, registered dietitian. They are listed in most phone books.
3. Unless you have a specific deficiency or medical problem, you probably don't need extra vitamins or other supplements.
4. However, if you are a heavy smoker or drinker, are taking birth control pills or heavy medication, you may be losing some important vitamins. Consult your doctor, dentist or dietitian about appropriate supplements.
5. If you do take vitamins, you should know that vitamins B and C are water soluble, and excess amounts will be excreted from your system in your urine. Others, A, D and E, stay around in fatty tissues and, if taken in megadoses, can cause problems.
6. Don't make a 180-degree change in eating habits. Change slowly so you don't damage your system.
7. Don't feel you have to eat all the food on your plate when eating out. Eat slowly, chew thoroughly and stop when you feel you've had enough.

The Protocol of Eating Out

Eating out can be great fun, and you will undoubtedly want to take the time to discover new restaurants and dining pleasures. But a lack of familiarity of restaurant protocol can make some people feel a bit less secure about the experience. The following tips are designed to answer some of those often unspoken questions.

1. *Make reservations.* Planning that big night out at an especially well-known or popular restaurant? Call several days to a week in advance for reservations. On weekdays and at less popular eateries, call half a day in advance. Many good restaurants insist on reservations. Avoid disappointment by calling ahead.

2. *Be on time.* That reservation may not be held, and you may have to wait an hour or more for the next opening, if one can be had. If you change your mind about the restaurant or the time, call and cancel or change the time.

3. *It is not necessary to tip the host.* Except under exceptional circumstances, where the host (known in better restaurants as the maître d'hôtel or simply maître d') has done you a special favor or provided you with an unusually fine accommodation, don't tip for this service. If you do so, do it on your way out and thank him orally at the same time. Leaving the customary tip at the end of the meal will suffice for the waiter, busboy, etc.

4. *Don't hesitate to send food back.* If your order is poorly or inadequately prepared, if it isn't what you ordered or is cold when it should have been hot, send it back. If there is a fly in your soup, hair in your cheesecake or the silverware is dirty, bring it to the attention of your waiter or waitress. Do so confidently but diplomatically. Don't make a fuss and cause embarrassment to the staff or your dinner partner. If the waiter doesn't immediately offer to rectify the situation, ask to see the host or the manager. Don't hesitate to exercise your rights, but don't make other patrons aware of your problem.

5. *The only excuse for returning wine is if it is bad.* To tell if the wine has turned, smell the damp cork. If it is dry, the bottle has been stored incorrectly. In this case, smell the wine before you taste it. If you think it may be bad, ask the waiter, wine steward or bartender to evaluate it. In any good restaurant, they will be more than fair, and if there is any doubt, the matter will be decided in your favor.

6. *Read your check carefully.* Make certain it is *your* check and that you received everything you were charged for. It is not "classy" or "sophisticated" to ignore this aspect of dining out. Next, add the check to see if your addition and that of the waiter agree. Waiters make mistakes like everyone else. If you feel there has been a mistake, intentional or otherwise, quietly bring it to the attention of the waiter and ask him to explain the error or make the correction.

How to Save When Eating Out

Depending on the restaurants, there are numerous ways to save when eating out, while still enjoying the evening and not feeling like a cheapskate.

1. *Avoid cocktails and wine.* (Remember, I'm providing ways to cut costs on eating out, not drinking out.) Many restaurants make more money on the alcoholic beverages they sell than on the food. Two or three drinks before and during a meal or one well-chosen bottle of wine could cost you as much or more than the food. Wine often is marked up as much as 200 percent from retail prices.
2. *Avoid desserts and coffee,* or at least desserts. A 25¢ cup of coffee can cost you $1.50, and desserts can cost up to $3.50 each (higher in major cities). Turning away a delectable dessert tray will benefit your waistline *and* your pocketbook.
3. *Order from the complete meal menu rather than à la carte,* if you want soup, appetizer and dessert. Skipping the preliminaries, it is usually cheaper to order from the à la carte menu. À la carte simply means that you can order each item separately at individual prices. If the menu doesn't list items à la carte, ask your waiter if you can order à la carte anyway.
4. *Split a dessert or an appetizer*; even an entree if you think it will be ample. A variation on this approach is to order two appetizers and no entree, but include dessert. You may get a disgusted look from the waiter, but he or she will provide what you ask, and it is another way to save.

5. *Read the menu carefully.* Note whether the tip or gratuity is automatically included in the check. If it is, the menu should say so. It should also state the percentage of the tip. While 15 percent is standard in most restaurants these days, it is not unusual to find a 20 percent gratuity at some of the more "posh" places where businesspersons eat on the expense account. It is not necessary to include the tax in figuring the tip.

6. *Determine whether the eatery takes credit cards and personal checks.* If that is unclear and you intend to put the bill on a card or pay by check, inquire from the maître d' before being seated.

Eating In

Eating at home can be a fun and challenging opportunity to learn new skills, improve your health, save money, make new friends and entertain old ones. Ot it can be a drag, expensive, time consuming, messy and simply a tiresome necessity. It will be what you want it to be.

Knowing how to prepare and serve food well long has been a sign of true sophistication and independence. The following are some helpful hints on keeping food costs down.

1. *Plan your meals for the entire week.* Then make a list of items you need to buy and *stick to the list*.

2. *Resist impulse buying.* It is the surest way to increase the cost of your food basket. Don't buy things you don't need.

3. *Never shop on an empty stomach.* This creates another form of impulse buying.

4. *Avoid the popular, nonnutritious snack foods.* They run up your food bill and add nothing but calories. If you must snack, try fruits, cheeses and crisp veggies.

5. *Buy large sizes of things that will not spoil.* Especially detergents and other cleaning supplies.

6. *Look for sale items and sale days.* Newspapers abound with

food store ads on Wednesdays since most people shop on Thursdays, Fridays and during the weekends.

7. *Shop early in the day to take advantage of availability and selection.* One exception might be shopping for produce on Saturday evening or even Sunday. New produce will be arriving on Monday, and you may be able to take advantage of markdowns prior to their arrival.

8. *Learn to use coupons.* Newspapers, women's magazines and the stores themselves use coupons to reduce prices and get you to try various products. They can be cost savers. But don't buy a reduced price product if it is not needed.

9. *Buy store brand or plain label goods.* Many stores are now offering such items as canned goods, dry package goods and the like at significant price reductions. The label is usually a single color and white and not done by an expensive ad agency. It will carry the required packaging information, however.

10. *Seek out food discount stores.* Many communities, especially in low to moderate income areas, are now sprouting discount stores. These offer the same items as larger supermarkets, minus the overhead—and conveniences. You will have to bag your own groceries and may have to pay a few cents for the bag.

11. *Consider a food cooperative.* This not only is a way to save money, but it also will give you a whole new circle of acquaintances. A cooperative allows a number of people with like needs to purchase more efficiently than individuals. And because the cooperative requires everyone to share the work load—picking up food at the wholesaler's, distribution and cleanup, for instance—you will have something constructive to do. You may also learn something about foods and wholesale operations as well.

12. *Shy away from the six-pack convenience approach to packaging.* The handy six-pack is far more expensive than the single large can or bottle. Price them next time you're in the store.

13. *Always comparison shop.* Compare stores, brands, frozen versus canned versus fresh foods, and individual portion

costs. The differences can be astounding. Start with cheaper items and see how you like them. Work up the pricing ladder until you come across a comfortable quality level.

Convenience Stores Versus Supermarkets

Food costs vary, depending upon where it is bought. Item for item, purchases made at so-called convenience food stores or neighborhood "mom and pop" shops cost more than at standard supermarkets. Resist the urge to patronize the smaller stores unless you are willing to pay for the convenience or are working hours that dictate that there is no choice. Then buy only what is absolutely needed.

Following is a list of twelve items priced at a supermarket and at a nearby convenience food store. The difference in total dollars spent is significant, as you can see.

		Convenience Store	Supermarket
1.	Box crackers	$1.39	$ .99
2.	Macaroni and cheese	1.46	.78
3.	Six rolls	1.12	.97
4.	One gallon milk	1.79	1.81
5.	One dozen grade-A eggs	1.05	1.05
6.	One roll toilet tissue	.69	.43
7.	Half gallon orange juice	.79	.85
8.	46 oz. vegetable juice	1.29	.89
9.	Cleaner	.69	.43
10.	One pound margarine	1.15	.89
11.	Regular drip coffee	2.99	2.49
12.	Pork and beans	.55	.33
	TOTALS	$14.96	$11.91

The cost difference is $3.05 or 25 percent greater expense at a convenience store. Over a year this can add up to big bucks.

There is another option worth exploring. The so-called "farmer's market" may or may not be less expensive. Those located in the country, especially the little roadside stands, can provide some real bargains.

Others calling themselves farmer's markets but located in major metropolitan areas or in suburban shopping centers usually have quality merchandise, and higher prices.

Labeling

1. *The contents of food packages or cans must list the ingredients in the order of their volume.*
2. *Perishable foods that are packaged should have an "open date" marking on them.* This means that the product is not to be sold after this date and that the store should remove it from the shelves. This does not mean the product is no good.
3. *Learn to compare prices by using "unit cost" labels.* These are usually found on the edge of the shelf, under the food item. Using a "unit measure" you will be able to determine comparative costs of various items that may be packaged in different-sized containers. If you know the cost for one unit (ounce, pound, liter, etc.) you are comparing like items.
4. *Labels must carry information indicating the calorie content and percentage of fats, carbohydrates and proteins.*
5. *Labels must note what the manufacturer has added,* including artificial colorings, chemical preservatives and artificial flavoring.

Buying Meats, Poultry and Fish

With the assumption that you are earning a reasonable wage for your age and experience and that this wage will not allow you to feast on filet mignon, lobster, pheasant and prime ribs every night of the week, here are some thoughts on purchasing meats, poultry and seafoods.

1. *Buy hamburger (or ground or chuck) in 3- to 5-pound quantities.* At home separate it into individual hamburger patties, wrap in freezer paper or aluminum foil, label, date and freeze it.
2. *Combine hamburger with cereals, breadcrumbs, vegetables (especially onions), eggs and other leftovers to make meat-loaf.* Cook it and keep it refrigerated and you'll have several meals. It is also good fare for when you have guests on short notice.
3. *Avoid "prime" cuts of meat.* They are expensive. Buy meats marked "USDA Choice." Most people won't know the difference between prime and choice.
4. *The butcher will help find something special or cut a piece of meat.* It won't cost extra.
5. *Buy a whole chicken if you don't mind the variety of parts* (legs, wings, breasts, gizzards, neck). One chicken will last one week, with a varied menu. Chicken remnants also provide the base for excellent soup. If you prefer chicken legs or breasts, buy the parts and don't waste the rest of the chicken.
6. *Shellfish (shrimp, scallops and lobster) are costly, so stick with fish.* Certain fish are more available locally. Test the waters. If you like them, you've acquired a new food preference; if not, try something else.
7. *Fish should be fresh the day it's purchased and should be eaten within a day.* Otherwise freeze it. Frozen and breaded fish are more expensive and often less tasty.

Whether looking for meats, poultry or fish, seek out the sales and the specials. Make certain they aren't leftover goods. If it smells funny or if it's contents appear to be turning color, reject it.

Buying Fruits and Vegetables

Fruits.   If you can buy fruit at a roadside stand or from a farmer, do so. It seldom will be cheaper in the store.

Learn when fruits become available. Apples are generally plentiful in the fall, oranges and grapefruit in the late winter and early spring, peaches and plums in midsummer, pears in the fall. Melons are midsummer fruit, as are grapes. Bananas and pineapples seem to be available all year round. *Avoid purchases at the very beginning of the season for each variety of fruit; the cost will be higher.* As the season peaks, the price will drop. Look for specials.

Fresh strawberries, cherries, blackberries and raspberries don't last long. Serve them the same day or within thirty-six hours. Most other fruits will last from three to five days, depending on storage conditions.

Vegetables.   Following are some helpful hints on buying vegetables:

1. Don't buy fresh vegetables to freeze for later use. Use them within a few days of purchase. Freezing vegetables removes some of the nutrients.
2. To slow the ripening of most fruits and vegetables, keep them in the refrigerator.
3. Keep mushrooms in the dark and let them breathe or they will turn dark and slimy.
4. Parsley should be kept moist in a bag in the refrigerator.

Freezing Things

There are some facts to know about freezing various items:

1. Buy frozen foods last on your list, then go directly home and stick them in the freezer. Don't permit them time to thaw.
2. If food thaws partially or completely, cook it. *Don't refreeze it.* It could become contaminated when thawed and refreezing does not destroy the bacteria; it preserves it. Food can be refrozen *after* cooking.
3. When freezing meats, poultry or fish, take them out of the plastic and cardboard wrappers and wrap them securely in freezer paper (you can find it at the store) or in aluminum

foil. Label and date the package. Hamburger should be separated into portions before freezing so that it is easier to use later.

4. Do *not* freeze fresh fruits, milk, sour cream, mayonnaise, egg salad, tuna, tomatoes, hard-cooked eggs or salad greens. Don't refreeze ice cream, frozen juices and meat prepared in cream sauces.

Storing Things

All fruits, except bananas, should be kept in the refrigerator. So should whole grains, they'll last longer. These store well in their plastic bags, but consider some attractive tin containers from the housewares section of your local department store. You also can get some jars with tight lids or refrigerator dishes in several sizes. Make sure the lids fit tightly. Air seeping into foods stored in the refrigerator will dry them out and cause unneeded waste.

Meats stored in the refrigerator (not the freezer) should be wrapped loosely so the air can circulate around them. Never store them in their plastic store wrappers for more than a day. Use them promptly.

Milk containers should be kept in the coldest part of the refrigerator. So should yogurt and sour cream.

Mayonnaise, chicken, tuna, ham, tomatoes, carrots, greens, hard-cooked eggs and cold cuts *should* be refrigerated. Keeping coffee, nuts and dried fruits in the frig will keep them fresher and make them last longer. The same holds true for bread, especially the natural breads without preservatives. French bread usually becomes stale in twenty-four hours if kept on the counter.

Potatoes, onions and squash should be stored at room temperature (better on the low temperature side) or in a cool, dry place with air circulation. There are plastic racks available in the housewares department at almost any discount store designed just for this kind of storage. They are on little legs and permit air circulation.

Check cake mixes, pancake mixes, corn meal and other powdery or grainy items kept in boxes. If there is a dust or sawdustlike substance on the shelf at the bottom of the box, it could have bugs. Examine it closely before using or throw it out.

Most apartments and many homes have bug problems at one time or another. It is a wise move to put small bags or boxes of flour, cake mixes, etc. in heavy plastic bags. This isn't going to get rid of the bugs, but it will make it more difficult for them to reach foods.

Don't store insect sprays, cleaners or deodorants near foods. If you store those items under the sink, don't store potatoes and onions there as well. And don't spray near foods of any kind, even packaged ones.

Making Food Go Farther

Many fresh foods will begin to turn brown, develop spots, get soft or wilt. But often they can be used or rejuvenated. For instance:

1. *If bananas are turning brown and mushy*, use them as a filler and moistener in any muffin recipe.
2. *When lettuce begins to wilt*, put it in sugar water for about four hours, then rinse thoroughly.
3. *When cooking vegetables, don't discard the water.* Save it to make soup or gravy. Otherwise, you'll be throwing out a lot of very nutritious vitamins and minerals. Freeze leftover veggies and use them in soup. A large plastic milk container is good for this purpose.
4. *When buying "choice" or "good" quality beef*, consider marinating it in red wine overnight before cooking it. Wine is a great tenderizer and will make the beef better as well. *Learn to use meat tenderizers* to make lesser quality beef easier to chew.
5. *Experiment with eggs*; they are inexpensive. Combine with veggies, diced meats, jams, spices and other stuffings for omelettes. Try poached eggs on corned beef hash. Scramble

with pieces of red pepper, Tabasco and Worcestershire sauces. Hot, but good!

6. *Buy dry or powdered milk.* Milk is expensive. Powdered milk, where you just add water, isn't. A box of instant dry nonfat milk will produce 10 quarts for $3.99. Ten quarts of regular skim milk (5 gallons) will cost $17.90. It may take a while to get used to the taste difference, but once you do, you'll be richer for the experience in several respects.

7. *Buy loose tea or coffee beans* rather than tea in bags or ground coffee. The cost difference can be significant; 16 ounces of instant decaf coffee can be as much as $8. Sixteen ounces of the grind-your-own variety cost $2.99 the last time I compared.

8. *Consider buying day-old bread* and refrigerating it. Day-old bread is reduced in price and can be found on a separate table in the store near the bread section. It should be so marked.

9. *Snack foods are expensive!* Sugar water with chemicals, otherwise known as soda, is also expensive. If you have to snack, substitute popcorn for potato chips, fruits for candy and loose granola or natural breakfast foods for granola bars.

10. *Don't hesitate to return items* you have purchased if they aren't right—meat that smells bad, cracked glass jars, cans that are bulging, a box of strawberries with the bottom ones inedible. Keep receipts; the store shouldn't give you any argument. And it is your right if you aren't satisfied with the merchandise.

9

Up Against The Wall: Building A Support System

The Need For Support

Most of us would like to think of ourselves as independent. After all, we make our own decisions. Oh, from time to time we consult with a friend or coworker. Perhaps we ask the guy down the hall about a place to get the car fixed, but *we* make the decisions. And that is independence. Or is it?

The fact is, we need others in more ways than we ever dreamed. We are dependent upon others for certain creature comforts, when we are in trouble, ill, victim of an accident, object of a legal suit, depressed and alone in a strange city. The requirement for support does not lessen the need for independence. Indeed, often we are part of another person's support system. That is, we are needed by someone else.

Networking

If a friend came to you and said, "Since you've worked previously in a restaurant, would you recommend restaurant management as a good career for me?" That person, by reaching out to you, would be employing networking. If you, in turn, say, "I'm not sure. Why don't I call so-and-so, the manager of the restaurant where I worked last summer, and see if he will talk to you," that's also networking. Networking is simply the interaction of people that creates a resource for information and contacts.

Don't hesitate to use networking! It is a valuable tool. People you know through your family or friends not only can be an important place to start in setting up your own network support system, they also can become your friends or business contacts.

Whether you are looking for a job, a date, a good place to take your parents to dinner, someplace to get discount tickets for a concert or a play or for a roommate to share expenses, you can reduce time and trouble, energy and cost, frustration and delay by exploring the networking concept.

Ann G.: "At first, when I was looking for a job, my parents urged me to use contacts they had, and I didn't do it. I was concerned that I might not come up to the expectations of these people, and it might reflect upon my parents. As time passed and I still didn't have a job, I swallowed my pride. Now I'm picking up the phone and calling people. I understand they aren't going to put their necks on the line, but I found if they can help me they will."

There are several kinds and levels of networking. One kind relates to your business or professional life. You will want to seek others who can be of help in developing your career. You also will have need for similar assistance on a personal basis. Within both your personal and professional lives, there are resources for people who are new to the community, business or profession, and there are those open only to people who have established themselves and are seeking another level.

For instance, as a management trainee, you may have to rely initially on a small network of other trainees. This can be broadened by periodically getting all the trainees together on an informal basis and inviting middle management people to meet with your group to share their experiences, from which you and your fellow trainees can benefit. It won't be long before your circle of contacts has broadened considerably. Just having exposure to additional people will help when advice and counsel is needed at some later date.

As you advance in your career, new networking opportunities will arise. Men will find the Junior Chamber of Commerce a place to meet other business people under thirty-five. Women will be exposed to the Business and Professional Women's Association. Professional associations exist in virtually every field, from accounting and advertising to sales and training. Membership usually requires at least one year on the job and a position beyond the training stage.

On a more personal basis, you can employ the networking concept through a variety of means discussed throughout this chapter.

Roommates

An early networking possibility is a roommate. To many people moving out on their own for the first time, the thought of having an apartment, decorating it as they choose and not having to be concerned with the foibles and peculiarities of roommates seems a blessing. Especially if, as one fellow put it, "I've had roommates for four years at school. I have no desire to have another for a long, long time." This attitude is understandable. But there is a practical side to having roommates as well.

THE POSITIVES

A roomate provides someone to talk to; someone with whom to share the burdens of the day; the joys of meeting someone special. They have a circle of contacts as well, and some of these people may become your friends and acquaintances. Having a roommate immediately increases the likelihood of broadening the number of people and resources to which you have access, while probably lessening any feeling of loneliness.

Joni S.: "I advise someone to obtain a roommate who is not necessarily a good, close friend. This way you each can go your own way, on your own schedule, without feeling that you have to do everything with the other person. I like my roommate, and she is ideal for me, but we respect each other's privacy."

Roommates share the rent and other costs. In smaller communities, where apartments usually are inexpensive, this may not be a consideration. But in New York, Houston, Los Angeles, Chicago or Boston, where apartments can cost in excess of $1,000 a month, few people on a starting salary can afford that kind of tab. A roommate may be a *must*.

If you're not ready to settle in one place, a roommate can also add to your independence:

Debbie G.: "I have lived in several different apartments. Each time I shared it with a roommate who already had the apartment. As a result, other than my bedroom furniture, I didn't have to supply anything. I still don't own any furniture to speak of, and best of all, because I have to move so often in my job, I've never had to sign a lease."

If any of the reasons mentioned in the previous several paragraphs make sense, consider a roommate. But know there are disadvantages as well.

THE NEGATIVES

If you are the kind of person who feels most comfortable alone, if you are a self-motivator, enjoy doing things on your own and can afford to live alone, you probably ought to do so.

With a roommate you give up a certain amount of privacy. If you've never had a roommate before, you may chafe at having someone around when you wish to talk privately on the phone, when dishes are dirtied and left in the sink, when the bathroom is occupied at an inopportune moment, when the roommate has a friend in.

Dividing the chores can cause a problem. Unless the room-mates agree who does the grocery shopping, cooking, cleaning, etc., joint living can be grating.

Betsy G.:   "I have an absolutely fantastic arrangement. We are both neat about our things and don't like a sloppy apart-ment. I was very interested in the decor of the apartment, and she didn't care about that at the time. I like to cook, and she likes to clean up afterward. It all works out really well. With my first roommate, it was just the opposite. It was a disaster from the start."

Another problem can be money. If a roommate is responsible monetarily, great. But if he or she overspends, is constantly late with the rent money, eats your food and forgets to replace it, runs up the phone bill and generally is financially irresponsible, you may find yourself on the short end of the bills and forced to be the heavy in collection of funds.

HOW TO FIND A ROOMMATE

"Single, white, female professional, seeks same to shr. 2 BR Apt. No smokers, pets or children. Call_____between 9 and 5."

One way to find a roommate is to advertise for one, if you have the apartment, or answer ads, if you are looking for one to share. The above ad ran recently in a Philadelphia newspaper. The best place to look for similar ads is in the weekend editions of daily papers or in local weeklies.

It's important to determine the kind of living arrangement with which you'll be happy. If you rent with people who party all the time and you enjoy reading in your spare moments, you should keep looking. Perhaps a single roommate, rather than several, would afford the quiet and privacy you seek, while providing the advantages of sharing.

Undoubtedly, you will want to interview prospective roommates. Since this kind of arrangement is unlike that of your college days, where people were thrown together, often with little choice, you can interview until you find someone or several people with whom you feel comfortable.

Find out what kind of work they do, how long they have been at it, whether they've shared apartments before and, if so, why they left. What problems did they have previously? What are they looking for in a roommate? Why do they want to share an apartment?

Are they morning or night people? Do they enjoy the same kind of music? Do they prefer cooking, eating or cleaning? Are they willing to put down a month's rent as a security deposit with you? (You had to with your landlord, why shouldn't a roommate?) Do they have furniture? Do they have pets? Special boyfriends or girlfriends? Any interests that would require space in the apartment? Are they homebodies or "goers?"

If you are a nondrinker and/or a nonsmoker, do they drink or smoke? Will they be around on weekends or away? Do they ski, jog, enjoy sports or play an instrument? Find out all you can about the individual or individuals and then determine whether the mix is compatible with you.

Another source of roommates is your workplace. If the company is large enough, the personnel or human resources department may well have a list of people who have apartments they might be willing to share. This can be an advantage or a disadvantage. You may wish to keep your personal and business lives separate, and rooming with someone from work, even if from another department, doesn't accomplish that.

A church, club, YMCA or YWCA connection may be helpful. A notice on the bulletin board or in the newsletter outlining your needs could turn up some interesting prospects with a common connection.

The alumni office of your alma mater also may be able to provide the name of someone residing in in your area. There is no harm in using a school tie if you have it.

In some large cities, there are roommate referral services. They are listed in the yellow pages under the heading "Apartment Sharing Services." In San Francisco, you find

Rentshare, along with three other agencies. In Chicago, there are no such services listed, but the District of Columbia directory includes four, with Affinity Associates and Roommates Preferred most prominent.

In Philadelphia, Sarah Loughran, head of Space Sharing Consultants, charges people with a place to share a flat $25 for the listing. People looking for an apartment to share are charged on a sliding scale depending upon the rental cost of the apartment. Fees run between $50 and $75. Sarah interviews all prospective roommates.

Meeting New People

Broadening our circle of friends and acquaintances is a common problem for most people, regardless of age, especially as we move into a new community. Fortunately, there are a number of tried and true methods you can employ.

Not every contact is going to turn immediately into a fast friendship or a lasting romantic attachment; it takes time to develop friends and acquaintances at whatever level. If, as you set about meeting new people, you are concerned about someone appearing uptight, shy or coming on too strong, give the other person some time to show his or her true stripes, just as you'd like them to take time to judge you.

Begin by taking stock of yourself. Think about all the things you've never done but thought someday you'd like to do: taking a photography course, learning to ride a horse, skiing, becoming an expert on French Post-Impressionist art or taking care of handicapped children, perhaps.

If you want to be a volunteer worker with a community service organization, look under that title in the yellow pages. In Chicago, you'll find no less than 800 community organizations that provide a wide range of services, from Alcoholics Anonymous to the Welfare League. In Memphis, there are 193 such agencies, and in Philadelphia, more than 440.

In addition to the various activities and organizations I've listed previously, there are some specialized groups that bear mentioning. If you are a woman, for instance, you may have an interest in Planned Parenthood, Right to Life, the Black Women's Forum, the Junior League, Women Against Rape, anyone of several lesbian groups or a battered or abused women's program. (Many of these activities go under different names in different cities. Use the yellow pages under the heading "Associations.")

In most cities, there is an assortment of foreign language, ethnic, or religious clubs and service organizations, in addition to those connected with churches and synagogues.

Among the many volunteer service organizations to which you may wish to donate time or avail yourself of are: American Civil Liberties Union, Amnesty International, American Friends Service Committee, Asian Human Services, Big Brothers–Big Sisters, Blind Service Association, United Cerebral Palsy, Mental Health Association, Recording for the Blind, the YWCA and YMCA, YMHA and YWHA and Volunteers of America, Inc.

In any city, there are free events. Check your local newspaper for specific information. On a recent weekend, my newspaper listed eighty-five things to do, of which thirty-five were free. At least a dozen more cost less than $1.50. They ranged from a Gilbert and Sullivan operetta to open houses at historic homes to art shows and old movies.

Think like a tourist. Take a sightseeing bus and talk to the person next to you. (She or he may be doing the same thing you are, for the same reason.) Walk and talk to people you meet along the way—to storekeepers, corner vendors, children, people sitting on porches and on benches in parks. Don't be afraid to smile and say hello.

Try a health club or a sports group. Many communities have sports organizations looking for adults who would like to learn to become officials. Yoga, jogging or running clubs abound. Theater groups are fun. Even if you've never acted in your life, you can paint scenery, move props or take tickets.

If you have some special talent, become an instructor. Teach swimming at the Y, backgammon at your church, computer sciences to children, French to travelers or dance to anyone.

If you are interested in gourmet cooking, Dixieland jazz,

weaving or tennis, hang around places where you are likely to
find people with similar interest. When you do, be bold. Initiate
the conversation. Perhaps the other person is as shy as you are
and would welcome the effort.

Try museums and zoos. Both can be fun, as well as good
places to meet others.

Join an extended family. Today, many religious groups try to
gather people of varying ages for social events so younger adults
meet surrogate grandparents, people with families have both
older and younger friends and their children have a full range of
adults to get to know and learn from. People away from home
develop a feeling of belonging to a kind of family unit, similar
but different from the one they came from. This kind of arrangement provides a place to go on holidays or at especially lonely
times. It is a marvelous arrangement for all concerned.

Bonnie B.:   "I grew up in a navy family. We moved often,
and everywhere we went, there was built-in support system of other navy people. It was like a small community.
When I moved to this area after my parents divorced, I
found it difficult settling in a non-navy community. For a
long time, I had a feeling of isolation. But eventually, I
found several groups oriented to the things of interest to
me. My first extended community was a yoga group. Yoga
deals with more than one level of human makeup. I also
found that a group with spiritual orientation might be a key
to developing a feeling of mutual support. And I found it
through the church I went to. Ongoing activities were important. There was always a place to be and a time to be
there. And even when I can't be there, it is a place to send
my love and sharing and thoughts. It gives me a good feeling to be part of something greater than myself."

The possibilities are endless, limited only by your willingness
to try new things. Just get yourself off your duff and into the
world.

When You Need Medical Help

Your stomach has been bothering you for several days. It has been accompanied by occasional sharp pain. You've brushed it off, thinking it would go away. But tonight, you are about to jump in the shower, anticipating an evening out, when the pain suddenly becomes intense. Frightened and alone, you call a friend or neighbor. After forty-five minutes, he or she arrives at your apartment and finds you looking quite ill. "We have to get you to the doctor," your friend states. But you don't have a physician. You've not had the need for one. What to do?

You were fortunate. You had a friend or neighbor to turn to. What would have happened if no one were available or you knew of no one to call?

The answers are relatively simple. First, make certain you have medical and hospitalization insurance, which can be obtained through your employer or an insurance company (see Chapter 7). Second, have a phone number for the nearest ambulance service or rescue squad. Third, find a doctor as soon as you arrive in your new community.

Finding a Physician

One of the first things you should do upon arriving in a new community is to find a personal physician and any specialists you may need. If you are a woman, you will want to find a gynecologist with whom you feel comfortable.

One way to do this is to ask the medical people who cared for you at home or school to recommend someone in your new community. The medical community is surprisingly small. It is entirely possible that your family doctor will know someone who he or she can recommend. If not, he will have a directory of members of the state or county medical association, which will list physicians who reside or maintain practices in the area where you now live. At the very least, he could contact a physician he might know who could make a referral to someone who could be of help to you.

Contact the county medical association. The yellow pages of

your phone book lists such groups under "Professional Associations" or simply "Assocations." In Wilmington, Delaware, for instance, you'll find "Medical Society of Wilmington" listed. You may have to do a little research to find the appropriate listing.

You can also look in the white pages under the county or city heading. Here you are likely to find Allegheny County Medical Society if you live in Pittsburgh, Dade County Medical Society if you live in Miami, and King County Medical Society in Seattle.

If you are looking for a physician, call the medical society during regular business hours and ask for a few names located closest to your home or place of work.

The yellow pages also lists physicians under that title and, in many communities, includes a listing of people who limit their practices to various specialties.

Many doctors will have several sets of initials after their names. In addition to MD (Medical Doctor) or DO (Doctor of Osteopathy), some will have FACS, for Fellow American College of Surgeons, or FACOG, Fellow American College of Obstetrics and Gynecology. This means they have completed specialized training, passed examinations that certify them as a specialist in the field and are board certified. Not all doctors are board certified, nor is there any reason they should be. A physician may have taken the training but elected not to take the examination for various good reasons. He or she then would be considered as board eligible.

There is a special designation for family practice physicians who are certified as members of the American Academy of Family Physicians (AAFP). However, many good doctors, general practitioners, for instance, are neither board certified nor eligible.

If you are looking for a specialist with board certification, again try the reference librarian. *The Directory of Medical Specialists* is available at most libraries.

Another source for locating a physician is a nearby hospital. Call the office of the hospital administrator and ask for the name of a doctor in your neighborhood who is associated with the hospital. If you are looking for a younger doctor or an older one, a woman or some other specific classification, ask in the office of the administrator for a couple of references.

Once you have obtained names of several physicians, contact them. Ask about the hospital they are associated with, whether they are in practice with several other physicians (so you are covered if he or she is not available when you need them) and if the doctors make emergency home calls. Ask whether they accept your medical insurance coverage and about the procedure for filing claims. Some doctors will accept the payment limit provided by the medical coverage and will process the claim for you. You do nothing. Others will insist on payment before leaving the office and will give you a receipt, which is filed with the insurer. In some cases the amount of the bill will be higher than the amount allowed by the insurer. You pay the difference. If you are part of a Health Maintenance Organization, the HMO will supply a list of participating physicians, and you pay the physician nothing.

Feel free to ask about charges. Any doctor should be willing to discuss fees, particularly if you are paying your medical costs yourself. This can be a major factor. Doctors, like businesses, often charge the rate the market will bear. It is not out of line to compare costs.

Medical Emergencies. You are lying on a gurney in a hospital hallway, awaiting help. The diagnosis from the emergency room doctor is probable appendicitis. Since you don't have a personal physician, you'll soon be admitted for observation and possible surgery. Your friend left, and you are, again, alone.

Because you had insurance, you were admitted to the hospital for observation and treatment. If you had not had such insurance (see Chapter 7), unless you were in a life-threatening situation, you might have been turned away. Today, few hospitals will admit a patient without insurance or proof of financial responsibility.

What constitutes an "emergency"? To get the answer to that question, I consulted the Thomas Jefferson University and Hospital, a medical teaching facility in Philadelphia with an excellent emergency room. Their answer was: If you encounter medical problems such as breathing difficulties, unconsciousness, uncontrolled bleeding, major burns, heart attack symptoms such as chest pains, spinal injuries, shock or possible poisoning, get yourself to an emergency room! If you believe your life may be endangered, for any reason, treat the situation as an emergency. Often, prompt action in treating a medical problem as an emergency can mean the difference between life and death.

Dr. Joseph A. Zeccardi, of the Jefferson staff, points out that in 1982, over 83 million patients were seen in emergency treatment facilities. He urges you to plan ahead for possible emergencies and suggests you know the phone numbers of a poison control center, rescue squad and local emergency facility. And in case you have to get yourself or someone else to the emergency facility, know how to get there by the most direct route.

I asked a physician friend, associated with a major metropolitan hospital, what advice he had for people in their early twenties, living away from home. He suggests they keep a thermometer in their apartment medicine chest as a key medical emergency indicator. People in their early twenties seldom run a temperature above 101 degrees. If they do, they should obtain medical assistance promptly, he cautions.

Keep a plastic ice pack in the refrigerator for emergency treatment of sprains or strains. Unlike ice wrapped in a cloth, this item is self-contained, won't drip, and as it starts to melt, it can be put back in the freezer for half an hour and refrozen. It is well worth the few dollars it costs.

If you are in need of any special medication or are allergic or sensitive to medication, keep this information on your person. A Medic Alert bracelet or necklace will help medical personnel if you are unconscious.

Medic Alert is a profit-making organization, founded in 1956. It sells small bracelets and pendants with medical information contained on the back. In the event you are incapacitated, anyone administering medical attention will know such things as whether you are a diabetic, are allergic to certain drugs or have other medical abnormalities. Medic Alert also will keep detailed medical records about you in their headquarters. A medical person can obtain access to those records in an emergency or if you are a great distance from home by calling Medic Alert toll-free, twenty-four hours a day. The lifetime cost to obtain full services including the necklace or pendant in stainless steel is $15, but the peace of mind is well worth the minor expenditure. Medic Alert is located at P.O. Box 1109, Turlock, CA 95381 or call 1-800-344-3226, toll-free.

If your needs are less significant and you only wish to alert someone that you have a medical condition in an emergency, you can purchase a simple bracelet or necklace at most drug stores for about $4.

FINDING A DENTIST

Some of the suggestions for locating and selecting a dentist parallel those for finding a doctor:

1. Ask for referrals from your dentist at home or school or from friends and acquaintances in your new community.
2. Look for people who may be connected with a dental school.
3. Consider a dentist affiliated with a clinic or practicing with several other dentists. This should provide backup care in an emergency or while the dentist is away.
4. Look for a dentist who is willing to discuss his fees, then compare.
5. Check the length of time it takes you to get an appointment. If it is more than a couple of weeks, the dentist may be overworked or have too large a practice for the kind of service you want and deserve.
6. Determine whether the dentist has a staff of assistants and hygienists. The dentist should do the serious work, with preparations handled by an assistant. Cleaning teeth, routine X rays and checking gums for potential trouble should be the responsibility of the hygienist. You may like your dentist to handle all these tasks personally, but these days, in an efficient dental practice, the less complicated procedures are handled by a staff person. Further, the service of the assistant or hygienist will cost less than the service of the dentist.

7. Be sure the dentist requests your dental records and your medical history before working on you. Some dentists will want to take a blood pressure test and virtually all will ask about potential allergies or sensitivity to various forms of painkiller.

8. Ask the dentist about his philosophy. You should be looking for someone who believes in and practices preventive medicine. Be cautious of someone who immediately wants to pull a tooth rather than restore it. Look for a dentist who understands and discusses the need for good nutrition, since faulty eating habits often show up first in the oral cavity.

9. If you need dental surgery, beware of a dentist who wants to put you under a general anesthesia administered in his office. A local anesthesia administered in the area where the work is to be done is generally safe, reliable and normal. But if you must have general anesthesia, insist on going to a hospital and on being introduced to the anesthesiologist beforehand. If your newfound dentist disagrees, consider switching dentists or, at the least, getting a second opinion. The reason? Most dentists are totally unequipped to administer and monitor general anesthesia, and it can be a dangerous practice.

Psychologists and Psychiatrists

There will be points in your life when you feel depressed or when you begin to suspect that the world is unraveling around you. This is hardly unusual. Most of us have had such feelings to one degree or another. When and if this occurs, there are trained professionals available to help.

If you feel you may have need for psychological or psychiatric care, have a thorough physical examination first. Make certain that your troubles aren't treatable from a medical standpoint. Many "modern" illnesses—hypoglycemia (low blood sugar) and PMT (premenstrual tension), for instance—can and are treated with programs of diet, exercise and some medication, yet the symptoms displayed by each might well lead someone to think he or she needed psychological help. The individual *might* need such help. But the advice of at least one psychiatrist is to discuss the matter with your family doctor or a qualified internist, have a good physical checkup and then, if the results still point to the need for psychiatric help, seek such through your physician's reference.

Finding the right psychologist or psychiatrist can be a more difficult task than finding a dentist or physician. The difference between a psychologist and a psychiatrist is one of degrees. The psychiatrist is trained first as a medical doctor and then, with additional training analagous to that required of a surgeon or opthalmologist, develops a specialty. He or she, by virtue of being a licensed physician, can then dispense drugs. A psychologist cannot.

A psychologist may have either a masters or a doctorate and is qualified to give and evaluate various mental tests. If a psychologist is also a therapist, he or she must have two years' supervised experience in most states.

Finding a psychologist is not a problem; like other professional services, they are listed in the yellow pages. Finding one with whom you feel comfortable and who is well regarded is a bit more difficult. Many psychologists practice as part of a clinic, with other therapists. Look for someone licensed. A fact-finding visit at no cost should be a must. Check costs and whether insurance will cover part of your hourly charge.

With a psychiatrist, you can look for board certification, but since this offers no information about individual characteristics, request a recommendation through another medical person. These days, many physicians maintain a professional relationship or affiliation with psychiatrists or psychologists so that they can refer patients to the specialist when needed.

Almost every major community has a mental health–mental retardation center. In some cases, it may be called the community mental health center. Here are trained psychologists and social workers who can often help get you out of the doldrums, make you understand your problems and provide names of counselors who can assist you on a long-term basis, if needed.

Control and licensing of psychological counseling services vary by state. In some, counseling must be under the direction, but not application, of a psychiatrist. In other instances, the director need only be a Ph.D. psychologist. In most circumstances, the person doing the counseling must hold at least a master's degree in psychology, counseling or social work.

The best advice I and others, professional and user, can provide is to seek recommendations. If you can, start with your family. If not, and if you have a clergyperson with whom you feel comfortable, ask for references there. You may wish to seek out your family physician and see what direction he or she may send you.

One final observation. Be certain you are dealing with someone in whom you have confidence and with whom you feel comfortable. If not, back away and keep looking.

Spiritual Support

While you are exploring and challenging new ideas, now is a good time, before settling into life's routines, to explore your religious beliefs, disbeliefs or indifference. Further, a religious affiliation with which you feel comfortable can expand your network and solidify your support system.

You may wish to seek out a religious institution similar to that with which you grew up, particularly if your early religious experience was satisfactory. If not, try different ones, from the liberal to the more conservative. I know of no institution that will turn you away if you are seeking information and understanding.

If applicable, and depending upon the level of interest, you might visit a different religious institution each Saturday or Sunday for several months. Get a feel for the differences and the atmosphere. Or if you want to get deeper into the philosophy and beliefs of just several, call the office of the church or synagogue and ask for an appointment with the minister, priest or rabbi.

Rick M.: "For the first year of so after leaving school I didn't give a thought to religion. Then one weekend, I think it was in the fall, I awoke on a Sunday morning and just felt I wanted to go to church. So I looked in the phone book for a Methodist church, since I had been brought up Methodist, and I went. Well, it stirred up memories and questions that had been lying there for a long time. Although I felt uncomfortable about the experience that morning, it launched me on an interesting journey over the next two years. I spent one evening a week for several months with a delightfully fascinating Jesuit priest. We became good friends, and I was really challenged in some of my thinking. But I found I couldn't embrace Catholicism. So I kept looking and finally found a church in which I felt comfortable. And with it, I found a lot of new friends—kind of an extended family, I guess."

When You Need Legal Help

There are as many different kinds of attorneys or lawyers as there are physicians. Sorting them out can take a little effort. For example, after reading about a well-known newspaper columnist who was forced to spend three days in jail because of some misunderstandings and bureaucratic foul-ups, I vowed then and there that I would always have available the phone numbers of a lawyer friend, just in case I found myself in a similar situation. I mentioned this to my lawyer friend several weeks later. He responded, "I'm flattered, but I'm a corporate attorney. I don't know the first thing about practicing that kind of law." Under the circumstances, he would have contacted another lawyer for me, but beyond that, he was helpless.

FINDING A LAWYER

Obviously, your best source of a lawyer is personal referral. If your family lawyer can recommend a friend, colleague or former classmate, so much the better. If not, the local legal reference service may be able to help. In most cases, this agency will have attorneys' names but won't be allowed to evaluate them.

Another source is the library, where you'll find a copy of *The Martindale Hubble Directory*. This several-volume publication lists every legal firm in the United States. Lawyers use it to find attorneys or law firms in other cities. In it, you will find several things: first, listings of law firms, with addresses and phone numbers; second, a rating by the attorney's peers; and third, the kind of law practiced by the attorney. (Sometimes a firm will buy a space in the book to advertise itself and its people. It might include schooling, law honors, clerkships, etc.)

Another source is the local bar association. Most cities of any size, counties and states will have a bar association. Each will have several committees. One will be on evaluation and accreditation. You can inquire about the chairperson of the committee and contact him or her for an assessment of the attorney you may be considering. What you are likely to receive is simply a "qualified" or "unqualified" statement, but occasionally, you might get a "highly qualified" response. You should also be able to discover the kind of law the individual practices to make certain the attorney's expertise matches your needs.

There are many attorneys who practice general law. They will handle wills, minor lawsuits, divorces, reviews of leases and other legal documents, etc. For the most part, this is the kind of all-purpose attorney you are most likely to need. But always explore the scope of his or her practice so you know what you can and should not expect.

Some attorneys specialize in tax work, others in real estate law. Many never see the inside of a courtroom or a police station. It may benefit you to deal with an attorney who has several other people in his firm so you can call on them when you need help in specialized areas.

Talk to the attorney you have in mind. Tell him or her what you are looking for. If the individual is particularly busy or too high on the legal totem pole to deal with your matters, he or she may refer you to someone else in the firm who would be delighted to have you as a client.

Rapport with your attorney is as important as his or her capability to practice law. You want someone with whom you feel confident and comfortable. Say you'd like to set up a meeting and ask about any initial fact-finding fee. There should be no charge at this time. In fact, a good lawyer should not demand a fee unless his or her services will be used.

Determine at this meeting whether your concern requires legal attention, whether there is another, less costly, way to handle it and whether you want to hire this particular attorney. Get an estimate of the cost based on the lawyer's time and the complexity of the case. In short, know what you are in for and what it is likely to cost before you agree to retain the lawyer.

If you pay the lawyer a fee up front and decide he or she is performing unsatisfactorily, you'll have a hard time getting any money back. Try employing the "pay as you go" approach, to which most lawyers subscribe.

Legal fees vary substantively as to the nature of the legal problem, the kind of practice, the size community and area of the country. However, there is a reasonable range of charges for most simple legal needs.

- Reading a contract, such as a lease—$50 to $100.
- Representation at a civil court hearing—$300 to $500.
- An uncontested divorce—$500 to $1,500.
- Real estate closing—$200 to $400.
- Defense in a criminal case—$30 to $100 per hour.

In any event, it is wise to obtain a cost estimate, *in writing*, before hiring an attorney. In more and more communities, legal clinics are sprouting up, often in shopping centers. Here, routine legal cases are handled at reasonable costs, often by newer, younger lawyers. They specialize in handling uncontested divorces, landlord–tenant disputes, simple wills, name changes, disability claims, contract reviews and disability claims. Cost for simple legal advice is usually in the $25 range.

For further information on this subject, contact: National Resource Center for Consumer Legal Services, 1802 18th Street, N.W., Washington, DC 20036.

Another new development in the field of law is a prepaid legal insurance plan, like health insurance. Obtained through many employers as an employee benefit, a fee is paid once yearly and the employee is provided at least partial payment of any legal costs incurred during the year. Further information can be obtained from: American Prepaid Legal Services Institute, 1155 E. 60th Street, Chicago, IL 60637.

IF YOU ARE ARRESTED

Suppose you find yourself behind bars or, at best, in a holding room at a police station. What can and should you do? Is it true that you are allowed only one phone call and that you could be incarcerated with killers, rapists, robbers and the like or thrown in a drunk tank with little or no recourse?

According to one Philadelphia lawyer, you'll be asked a number of questions, but all you are required to provide the arresting authorities is your name and address. Regardless of the reason you're brought into the police station, it's better to say nothing until you have legal representation.

If you are arrested, you have certain rights. Whether the authorities grant those rights is another story. Once you are being held in detention, prison or jail, officials have the power to make rules, enforce them and prescribe punishment. Prisoner rights are good in theory, but in practice, the detainee, the individual charged, held but not tried and convicted, is often in worse circumstances than the convicted felon.

Prisoners being held for arraignment or pretrial hearings often are kept in overcrowded, unsanitary conditions with little or no protection. Despite first amendment rights, which say you have the right to speak to someone to obtain help, that right may be denied.

Technically, an individual has the following rights:

- To be free from cruel and inhuman punishment;
- To be able to correspond with lawyers, courts and legal-assistance agencies;
- To be free from sexual assault;
- To receive visitors;
- To receive health care and food.

The prison authorities have the right to review your mail in most instances, restrict your movement and set and enforce prison rules to search you and your belongings—and this includes a "strip search," including body cavities. Authorities have the right to deny medical treatment if, in their judgment, it isn't necessary.

In short, even though you may have rights, the prison authorities have the power.

Two excellent small books deal with your legal rights in clear, concise terms. They are:

- *Your Legal Rights*, by Linda Atkinson, Watts.
- *The Rights of Prisoners*, by David Rudovsky, Discus/Avon Books (available through the A.C.L.U.).

Kim E.: "Being arrested and knowing you are going to jail is a frightening experience. I have been in jail many times—local, county, city and federal. [Kim is a peace activist and has been arrested for various demonstrations against war and nuclear armament.] The most important thing is to stay friendly and open and not be hostile and troublesome. At the same time, you can calmly and in a nonthreatening way insist on your rights. I've had some very good responses. After all, the law enforcement people are human beings, too. But I've also had some bad ones. Each time I was arrested, I was booked, that is, fingerprinted, photographed, told what I was charged with and given a trial date. Sometimes, I was allowed to make a phone call and sometimes I wasn't. Sometimes, I was read my rights and sometimes not. The authorities can find ways of skirting your legal rights if they want to."

Depending upon the circumstances, legal troubles are either criminal or civil. A criminal suit involves an alleged breaking of federal state, city or local governmental laws. There are three levels of criminal law; felony, misdemeanor and summary offenses. In the former, if convicted, you are liable for a fine and/

or imprisonment for more than a year. In the case of a misdemeanor, the jailing usually is for less than a year, and the fine is minimal. In both cases, guilty or innocent, you have an arrest record. In the third, a summary offense, the charge usually is a minor one, such as a parking or moving traffic violation. Here you pay the fine, if guilty, and you have no criminal record.

For criminal charges, in most jurisdictions, you may elect to have a court-appointed attorney represent you. In smaller communities, this could be a problem since there may be no court-appointed attorneys. In this case, you would have to hire someone, but if you are of legal age and possess no monetary resources, you can ask for an attorney to be appointed by the court. In most major cities, this individual comes from a pool of lawyers usually called voluntary defenders.

The second major kind of suit is civil. Here you have broken no law of the land and thus have not offended the people. You have offended some individual or corporate entity. This kind of lawsuit would arise from breaking a lease, from an insurance claim or as a result of an accident you may have caused by carelessness, for example. This is the most common type of legal suit.

Many job application forms ask if you have ever been arrested. Not convicted, just arrested. If you have been arrested on either a felony or a misdemeanor charge, you will have a record and you'll have to confess same on your application. If you have a summary arrest or conviction, there is no record.

If You Are a Victim

Another legal matter about which we should be aware is our rights and options should we become crime victims or witnesses. Fortunately, there are governmentally sponsored programs to help lead us through this maze, generally without having to engage legal counsel. Most states have what is called a victim assistance program or victim/witness assistance program. The National District Attorneys' Association, 666 N. Lake Shore Drive, Chicago, IL 90911 has a booklet that provides information about these programs and lists program offices in various cities.

However, any victim has the following rights:

- Not to be intimidated;
- To be told about social services agencies that can be of help;
- To be assisted by your local criminal justice agency;
- To be told about any available compensation.

About one-half the states have a crime victim compensation plan in which funds are provided to help the victim pay for expenses that might be incurred as a result of criminal action against the victim.

10

The Tie That Binds

Beyond the practical aspects of "movin' on out"—learning to set up and use a budget, finding a place to live, taking care of yourself if you are ill—there are some more personal aspects of leaving home. For most people, leaving home means creating an irreversible separation between yourself and parents or others who have been close to you. It means your relationship will never be the same.

And, for what comfort it may be, this is as it should be. It is normal. In a very real sense, the past years have been spent in preparation for this moment, no matter how hard it may be to accept for all concerned.

Great Expectations

What do you expect out of your newfound freedom?

Barbara S.: "I couldn't wait until I had an apartment of my own. I would be able to decorate it as I wanted to. I

wouldn't have to pick up my clothing or do the dishes if I
didn't want to. And I could come and go whenever I
wanted. All that was true, but there were many times when
I missed being home. It was not an easy transition for me."

Whether your expectations are grandiose or mundane, whether
you are anticipating being a world-beater or simply trying to get
away from whatever you didn't like at home, this move is one of
several in a long line of logical steps.

Many people, like Barbara, have found once they have what
they were searching for it isn't what they anticipated at all. This
holds true on many levels. The individual who longs to reach a
certain rung in the corporate structure often finds the reality of
the position anticlimactic. An "is that all there is?" feeling sets
in.

An actor or actress yearns to land that "special" role. When
success comes, it often brings wealth, fame . . . and loneliness.
Now they are public figures, often less independent than when
searching for stardom.

There will be times to exult in newfound freedom, but there
will be moments when the warmth and comfort of home begin to
look pretty good. Good as they may look now and then, the
change has been made; there is no turning back the clock.

Putting Things in Perspective

It is important to put this dichotomy in perspective. Life can and
probably will be better than it had been in certain respects. But
one set of interests and concerns will be substituted for another
and a certain amount of independence traded for new options.

Now there is the satisfaction of being able to earn a living,
balanced, on the other hand, by having to budget to meet increased financial obligations.

You now have the pleasure of making fettucini Alfredo yourself, while no longer enjoying the luxury of having the evening
meal prepared.

Now there is an opportunity to develop new skills, interests

and knowledge, lessening dependence upon others while increasing self-sufficiency.

That's what is meant by getting things in perspective. For
each new opportunity, there are a series of options and trade-
offs. To understand that is to develop perspective. We can sor-
row over the loss of one opportunity or rejoice over the acceptance of a new one. The choice is ours.

Life may not be exactly as we anticipated. But by looking for
new opportunities, taking advantages of new experiences, exploring new options and learning from our mistakes, we can go a
long way toward creating a new world where we gain self-con-
fidence and look forward to each new day.

Making the most of our opportunities and options will require
the development of three personal characteristics: calculated
risk taking, managing change and learning to resolve conflicts.

Risk Taking

Risk taking doesn't mean you have to drive a Formula One race
car or wander through a dangerous neighborhood in the dead of
night. It simply means having the courage to try something
about which you know relatively little. It would be a risk to go
off on a singles' weekend alone. The risk of rejection would be
high. But most of us have been able to make a few friends and to
get along passably in most social situations; why not at a singles'
weekend? Further, if you are feeling this way about it, isn't it
likely that some other people are feeling the same way? They
might be a bit nervous and have taken risks as well. It is a chance
worth taking.

There are all kinds of risks; most aren't as bad as we anticipate
they will be. The biggest risks most of us take are social. Will our
coworkers like us? Will we meet some people with whom we can
play a friendly game of bridge or explore the city from time to
time? There are nice people everywhere. It may take a little
effort on your part to find them, however.

Managing Change

Managing change can be another roadblock. Change has already
dictated that you are going to live somewhere different, are

going to a first job, will be living apart from family and friends. Almost every encounter will require change. One can fight it and become unhappy or adjust to it and be happier.

Much change is presented with options. You didn't *have* to accept that job or rent that apartment. It could have been closer to work. You could have turned down a date for Saturday evening. Change has been managed successfully in each situation. You will be able to do it in more complicated circumstances as well.

Look at change as an inevitable process. Accept the thesis that "the only constant is change," and changes, as they occur, will be easier to deal with. People who resist change, in my experience, frequently are unhappy. There is no way we can bring back "the good old days," and often, the good old days were more old than good anyway, if the truth be known.

Part of growth and one way to make life more exciting and enjoyable is to embrace change and use it to our advantage.

There certainly are going to be times when change isn't to our liking. If a job were to be lost, a loved one should leave, a fire engulf the apartment house or a serious illness strike, you would have to deal with negative change. Even out of these experiences can come some positives.

If a job is lost, it may be possible to engineer a new one at more money or in a better location. If a loved one leaves, you may find inner strength you never knew existed while coping with it. If a fire destroys your belongings, you can replace them with items more to your liking. There generally are positive sides to any negative situation, even though they may not be easily recognized at the time. Often they must be sought out and capitalized upon.

How change is handled is important to our overall well-being. But best of all, it is something that only we can handle. We have the power to make change work in our behalf.

CONFLICTS

Resolving conflicts is the third aspect of personal growth. At home, to some degree at school, there always was someone to take over in the event of conflict; someone to assist in resolving it.

Now that you are an independent adult, most conflicts will have to be handled by you alone. True, there may be legal problems where we seek an attorney and business conflicts handled by a supervisor, but the bulk of conflicts in our daily lives will be resolved by us and the persons with whom we are in conflict. How well these conflicts are handled will be a measure of our adultness and emotional maturity.

The keys to resolving most conflicts are calmness, a nonemotional approach, an open mind, reason, logic, facts, firmness and a willingness to compromise.

Is creating a conflict worth the effort? What options are there to resolve a potential conflict? How inconveniencing will it really be? Is it worth making an issue out of the matter? It takes two to make a situation a conflict. If it isn't a conflict for you, it isn't a conflict for anyone.

Aloneness and Loneliness

In reality, few of us have the inner resources to exist primarily in aloneness. Many of us do because, for various reasons, we have no other choice.

The widow or widower who has no children or other close relatives, the renegade who has trouble adjusting to society's rules, the individual who cannot handle change, the taking of risks or conflict all are examples of people who frequently have no choice. But most of us have a choice, and although we may choose to experiment with various living arrangements over the years, including living alone, we generally find that we are more comfortable living with others.

While living with others presents the potential for conflict, it presents as well the opportunity for shared intimacy, for love, appreciation and support, for affirmation of purposes and encouragement. Living alone can't provide those things. There is no one there to observe and recognize your needs, to acknowledge your successes and comfort you in your failures.

Doris J.: "After two years of living alone, I thought I'd go nuts. I had my fill of living with others in school, I thought.

But never having anyone to talk to, of always coming home to an empty apartment made me want to seek a living partner. At the same time, I was hoping I'd meet a man with whom I might develop a serious relationship. It just didn't work out. I may or may not find a man I like and who likes me, but I just can't take living alone anymore."

Doris's case is not at all unusual. All our lives we are thrown in with others: growing up in the home of our parents, at school, at work or play. Team sports are stressed over those entered into individually. Togetherness is emphasized in advertisements, in movies and on TV.

We tend to feel sorry for people who are alone. Our hope for them is to be part of a group, even if we are not happy in our group. How many marriages are there where, despite the unhappiness, living alone is seen to be an even worse fate?

Many of us prefer to live with others because we do not understand *how* to live alone. Or we do not have the kind of interests that are conducive to living alone. Often our support systems are such that it would be difficult and inconvenient to live alone. Probably the most prominent reason most of us live with others is because we fear being lonely. And in this feeling, most of us have not learned to separate aloneness from loneliness.

Being Alone

One of the most important things that can be taken from this book is the distinction between being alone and being lonely. It is true that one can be both, but being alone does not necessarily mean being lonely as well.

Aloneness does not mean becoming a hermit or reclusive. It simply means having time alone with nothing but our own inner resources to direct our efforts, fill our time and decide our next moves.

Perhaps that next move is to do nothing. That's OK! Perhaps it is to practice a musical instrument or read a good book. That's OK, too. I am alone as I write this book. There is no radio, no TV, no family member around to redirect my thoughts. Yet, alone as I am, I do not feel lonely, as I am engaged in something I enjoy and find emotionally stimulating.

RECOGNIZING LONELINESS

There are two basic levels of loneliness. The first is temporary and is with most of us from time to time. It comes and goes, depending upon what is confronting us. This is normal and controllable. The second is more serious in that it is more lasting. Fortunately, it affects fewer of us, but at the same time, when it does, it is harder to get rid of and is more deeply ingrained.

The former can be treated as we confront it. The latter needs to be dealt with by professionals.

Loneliness is a feeling that generally comes as a result of some change in our environment. A move to a new community, a new job, the death of a family member, breakup of a love affair or a marriage—all of these events can trigger feelings of loneliness.

And the feelings are manifested by bewilderment, a state of emptiness, aimlessness, a lack of sense of direction and, at times, an inability to make decisions.

These manifestations create changes in our regular personalities. Coworkers or family members, roommates or friends, begin to notice changes in our personality. These would include apathy, different eating habits, fatigue, hostility, irritability and a feeling of loss of self-identity.

Many people leaving school and going out in the world have periods where they experience these feelings. They are leaving a comfortable environment, one where they are known and have a support system, and starting anew—new job, living arrangements, friends and acquaintances, style of living, responsibilities. For some, the adjustment is easy. For most of us, there is some stumbling. And for a few, the road is rocky, the loneliness real.

As a result of loneliness, at any age, we turn to various, often less than satisfactory, solutions. One attempt at finding a solution is in eating—turning to the refrigerator or cupboard. For others, it is to get out and drive around, often spending long hours at shopping centers. Sometimes, it is going on a spending spree; a new outfit or some new clothes will surely help us "pep up" a bit. For others, it is refuge in alcohol, drugs or sexual activity. The negative results of bouts with any of these temporary solutions often are more pronounced than the initial lonely feelings. They often approach or reach a state of depression.

All of the research I have done on this subject indicates that each of us experiences temporary, or situational, loneliness at various times. Your parents likely will have encountered some form of it when you decided to leave home. The point I am making here is that situational, or temporary, loneliness is a normal occurence.

One reason many people leaving home feel lonely is because the relationship they have had with their parents is changing. As part of normal development as an independent individual, you are casting aside the day-to-day contributions of parents, and armed with little more than your native intelligence and what you have been taught by them and in school, you are facing the world. The difficulty is that most people "movin' on out" retain some emotional dependence upon parents.

Most of us miss the total acceptance and support of parents, even as we thirst for independence. The result can be a form of loneliness.

CONQUERING LONELINESS

To conquer loneliness, it has to be faced head on. There has to be understanding of what it is, what triggers it, that we needn't "escape" from it and that it can be turned around and made useful.

Like most things worthwhile, it takes time to develop an attitude that allows this. But we have to start somewhere, at some time. Next time a period of loneliness is coming on, accept it and acknowledge that you can control it. Then begin to do so.

First, tell yourself it is OK to feel lonely, that most people have the same feelings from time to time, that it is part of life and can be overcome with constructive and confidence-building steps.

These periods can be used to do things that will increase

feelings of self-sufficiency. Consider them as opportunities for growth and learning. By developing inner resources, we create a belief in our own ability to function in virtually any circumstance, thus lessening the feeling of dependence upon others, which makes us lonely when others are not present.

Let me be clear. I am not advocating seeking to divorce ourselves from any need for others. I am simply suggesting that self-sufficiency and a feeling of self-worth can help us through periods that otherwise could be crippling.

Specifically, how can loneliness be dealt with? One way is to avoid having empty time. An evening where the plan is to read or to research options for a vacation or to listen to Beethoven may seem to be nonproductive, but it has been developed to some purpose. Purposeless and aimless time lead to loneliness.

What triggers loneliness? It may be coming home to an empty and quiet apartment. Perhaps it is because the apartment seems so temporary, and it doesn't have the warmth of home. The answer may be to add some touches that make it distinctively yours, such as an inexpensive electric timer to turn on a light and the radio so the place seems cheery when you arrive. Environment is a major contributor to one's happiness.

Physical exercise is a good way to get rid of feelings of loneliness. Perhaps now is the time to begin an exercise regimen. An ideal time to exercise is immediately upon arriving home from work. This is when we are decompressing and often feel tired. Exercise, a shower and a change of clothing can make an enormous difference. It will get the blood running and likely make you feel ready to channel new energies into something constructive.

Another way is to get to know the community. Part of the reason people feel lonely in a new community is that it is not familiar. When landmarks, streets and stores become familiar, we immediately feel less lonely. If you eat out regularly because it is lonely eating alone, try one or two small restaurants and get to know the owner or the waitress or waiter. They'll begin to look forward to your arrival and will provide a friendly face.

In getting to know the community, learn about the history of the area, how parks got their names, who the community leaders are and something about the political system. Get to the point where you can give friends or parents a tour of the area when they come to visit and feel confident and knowledgeable in the process. Doing the reading to find that information will help fill the hours, and soon, you'll begin to feel "at home."

In Chapter 9, I mentioned numerous activities designed to develop things to do and people to meet. One of the surest cures to loneliness is to immerse yourself in something you like to do. It provides a purpose and meaning.

Watch your health. If you don't feel well physically, the emotional side can and will suffer as well. To help assure physical health, eat properly. Many emotional problems can be alleviated by proper nutrition. So don't scrimp on food or overeat.

Finally, don't live in the past. A constant desire to return home on weekends, to seek out old familiar haunts, to see old friends rather than to build a new life is not a healthy way to handle loneliness. Sooner or later, old friends will be gone or you'll have increasingly less in common. Old hangouts won't seem the same. New surroundings in a new community should replace them. As novelist philosopher Thomas Wolfe once stated, "You can't go home again."

ALONENESS AS A POSITIVE FORCE

Loneliness and being alone are not the same. One can be lonely in a crowd. At the same time, one can be alone and be far from lonely. It can be tremendously rewarding, productive and a source of great strength.

To be able to take advantage of the regenerative powers of aloneness, we must first appreciate the value of being alone. Because we so often conduct ourselves in a manner that we think others want us to, we begin to feel a need for the approbation of others to feel worthwhile. If no one is around to validate our existence and worth, we tend to lose confidence in ourselves. In reality, the thing that makes us most worthwhile is our own feeling of self-worth. If we don't have a feeling of self-worth, how can we expect others to consider us worthy?

The Parents' View

When we leave home, a set of parents or, in an ever increasing number of cases, a single parent, is left behind. While quite naturally, concern is with our own development, we should be aware that leave taking can be and often is a major event in the lives of our parents. And depending upon whether you are an only child or the first or last of several children to leave home, a departure creates a void in the life of one or more people who have been closer to you than anyone else has. It helps to understand what they are experiencing.

Most people leaving home come from two-parent households. Regardless of the parents' attitude about your leaving, they have each other and perhaps other children to whom they can direct attention and affections. It may be easiest on two-parent households to cope with leaving. At the same time, the individual leaving may have been all that was holding the parents together. In many divorce situations, the statement is made, "We elected to stay together for the sake of the children." A departure may mark the time of separation for parents both from you and from each other. *The thing to guard against is a feeling of guilt that the divorce or separation was caused by you.* Remember, parents are adults with powers of reason and the benefit of experience. They made the decision, not you. They are the people who elected to separate. They made the decision to stay together "for the sake of the children." You will have to evaluate their decision and deal with their separation, but don't allow yourself to be subjected to the burden of an unnecessary and unrealistic guilt trip because of their actions.

A majority of two-parent families will cope well. Some, recognizing that their days of responsibility are over, will welcome the addition of another adult into their world, and the event will bring with it a degree of relief. They now will have time for things that they might have had to reject previously—that special vacation, getting to know each other again or some form of recreational activity that previously was out of their reach.

Some will fight your leaving, particularly if you are an only child or the last to leave home. A mother who had devoted her whole life to raising her children may feel empty, lost, lonely and without value or meaning when her last child leaves the nest. These are likely to be difficult times for her if that is the case. And you will have to be especially understanding, while being fully aware that you now have your own life to lead.

Some parents will capitalize on the fact that their offspring are used to a certain dependence and will seek to extend that dependence.

Ginny R.: "I have a friend who has been working and living on his own for two years, but his mother still supports him. He doesn't choose to live on what he makes, so his mother sends him money every month for whatever he needs. That's hardly being on your own in my book."

Economic dependency is one of the toughest forms of dependency to break. Where you may be able to find sources of support for other needs, few people are going to bail you out when the need is for money.

Some parents continue to provide money well after the child has become an adult and has left home. Parents provide interest-free loans to children, lump sum gifts for the purchase of a home, financial support for a variety of activities and then, often subtly, pull in the strings by requesting that the individual spend more time with the parents, call home more often or write more regularly. Independence to these parents extends only so far. And the children, now young adults, perpetuate the dependence by accepting the largesse.

I know of one instance where a couple, aged thirty-six and forty, both working, with no children, needed a new heating system. The father of one member of the couple offered to pay for the installation. No strings were attached, but there was no question that the couple felt a certain obligation, because of the gift, to accommodate the father. And because of the implicit obligation, a certain amount of resentment existed as well.

Another favorite parental gambit to hold offspring is to threaten to cut the younger individual out of a will. At whatever age, this kind of parent will use whatever vehicle can be found to avoid allowing the child to become totally independent and to perpetuate the parent–child relationship. But the relationship can only be developed and continued on that plane as long as the child allows it. The answer, as it has been throughout this book, is that the choice is yours. You cannot be dependent if you do not allow yourself to be dependent.

The child can be replaced in the life of the parent by becoming an equal, a young adult, who can become a good and fast friend. It may not be an easy job. In fact, the parent may have to be persuaded that this is the kind of relationship you prefer, with the explanation that they are not losing but gaining in the process.

Perhaps the most difficult break is between an only child and a single parent. Often the single parent feels he or she has nowhere else to turn. He or she then is in the same position you are when leaving home—starting anew, lonely, in need of new friends, interests and directions. But because of the age of the parent and the single status in what is primarily a world of couples, the parent, less resilient and less resourceful, is faced with fewer apparent options. At this point, the roles of the parent and the child often begin to reverse. You will need to decide whether and how you can influence the life of the parent.

Females frequently encounter a special set of problems. Parents have a tendency to see the little girl whose hand they held on that first day of school. They likely will have gnawing doubts as to whether you have been sufficiently prepared to enter adulthood, feeling somewhat guilty that they might not have contributed enough to that preparation. There are likely to be tears and the need for constant reassurance that "everything is all right." Going to school or to work nearby with appeals to come home often, will be very much in the forefront of their thinking. Yet, you will have to prove that living independently can be done, that no harm will befall you, that you have become a competent adult.

Betty G.: "I think my mother had some difficulty with my leaving home to go to school. She really didn't want to let go. And it wasn't quite so bad while I was in school, but when I left again, after I had finished school and lived at home for a few months, she kept wanting me to come back home for meals and weekends. I must admit that when I first got my apartment, I still looked to my parents when I found myself in need or in trouble, but now I'm solving my problems myself. I think my parents, especially Mom, still have trouble adjusting to my being gone. They understand it intellectually, but it hasn't been a clean cut."

A few parents will welcome your leaving. Not because they want to get rid of you, but because they realize that the leave taking is a part of growing up. Sure, there will be an emotional tug; they will miss you. But they have accepted the departure as part of the web of life; they have done their job and feel good about it. If they are smart, they will welcome and enjoy their new adult friend and only occasionally will they revert back to the parent/child relationship. And with the healthy approach they have taken, those few regressions can be excused and, on occasion, even welcomed. After all, you will always be your parents' child, at whatever age. That is an inescapable fact.

Returning Home

There may come a time when, for whatever reason, you will want to return to live in the home of your parents. How you handle this situation will be of major importance. For the overwhelming number of people, the move will be temporary. If that is the intention, you and your parents must keep this in mind from the beginning. If it is your wish to return home for good, that is something that should be negotiated with them.

Depending upon how long you have been away, the return could well be a significant disruption in the lives of parents and/or siblings. If, for instance, a younger brother or sister has taken what used to be your room, the sibling may be unhappy and resentful at the thought of being dispossessed. Parents may have adjusted to a new lifestyle and may not want to readjust it to accommodate an unexpected homecoming, particularly if your arrival means an added financial burden.

On another front, your parents may request that your lifestyle

conform to theirs in some ways. This could seriously dampen
your social life after having been used to a freer and more independent existence. They may wish to impose the same restrictions you lived under in high school or college. Yet you have
been used to setting your own standards, more flexible or liberal. And in any event, you should hardly be treated as you were
in college or high school. You have become an independent
adult; conflict inevitably ensues.

If the returning home is because you believe you truly are
needed, carefully examine the rationale for this move. Do they
really need you at this time or is this a way of making yourself
feel needed? What are the true motives for returning home to
care of them? Make certain you are doing so without any feeling
of guilt or resentment. Either will manifest itself at some later
date, and not only will you be unhappy at lost opportunities, but
parents will be aware that the effort is not out of unselfish love
but for other, less valid reasons.

Not all homecomings produce troubled situations. There will
be adjustments on both sides, but most of the adjusting will have
to be made by you. Make it clear why you have returned. Set a
time for your next departure and outline a plan to make that
departure possible. Those steps will reduce parental anxieties.

After laying the groundwork, make it clear that you are willing
to accept responsibilities for certain activities around the home;
to share the load. Volunteer to mow the yard, clean up after
meals, take care of your own laundry, etc. At the same time,
establish your independence. Remember, you are a contribut-
ing adult, a temporary resident, not a child resuming a permanent residency.

To help establish that condition, pay for room and board, even
if it is a token amount. Most important, make it clear that this is
a temporary move and that you are working toward a specific
departure point. This will make living at home a healthy, balanced experience, both for you and for your parents.

The Cord Is Cut

I asked several young men and women when they felt the cord was cut, when they first began to feel they were no longer an extension of their parents' living arrangement. Some didn't know; they hadn't discovered the point yet. A few said when they married they would feel that way. Perhaps the one response that struck me as being most telling, was the one advanced by a man who said, "When I returned home one weekend to find that there no longer was 'my room.'" He explained that his mother, after about a year and a half, had turned his room into a guest room, taking the little personal things that had made it "my room" and packing them in boxes. The room no longer had any indications of who once had lived in it. "I knew then that I would always be welcome, but that this was Mom's way of saying, 'You're on your own now.' It hurt a little, but I knew it was coming sooner or later. I just didn't know when or how."

I know of no one who said he expected that leaving home would be easy, that there would be no trials and tribulations, no problems. You undoubtedly have confronted some or will confront them soon, if you are about to leave. But this is the stuff of life. That we are able to deal with them, learn from them and grow and change into whoever we really are is a sign of growth, and it should be exciting.

It is not easy to change something that has been so much a part of you for so long. But by leaving home, by the physical act of "movin' on out," you have indicated your intention to join the world on an equal footing, with an acceptance of the responsibilities and the benefits that independence dictates. The essential ingredient in how well that move is made is in how well the symbolic umbilical cord that binds you to your parents is cut.

They will always be your parents. That is a fact that can't be ignored or denied. How well this new relationship with them goes will, to a large degree, determine how well you will be able to function as an independent adult. If you cling to them long after the cord should have been cut, your development will be limited. Total separation eliminates a significant part of your new and broadened support system. A middle ground will have to be found, one that hopefully will prove to be satisfactory for both you and them, one that will allow their freedom and yours and yet retain the best of your very special relationship, without the strings and strains.

This book was conceived and developed with the hope that it will provide some guidelines and thought-provoking commentary to assist in setting up your new world. I hope the recollections of others, recounted from time to time throughout the book, have been beneficial and helpful. There is much that can be learned from others who have shared common experiences.

Severing a tie seldom is a happy experience, though it need not be deeply traumatic and negative. The symbolism of the cord, that life-sustaining link to your primary support system these many years, is valid. But just as the cord was literally cut at birth, releasing you from a certain kind of dependence, so, too, is the symbolic cord being cut now. You have reached a new level of independence with all the potential that it offers. Now, go for it!

Index